God at Work

Focal Point Series
ReViewing the Movies:
A Christian Response to Contemporary Film
by Peter Fraser and Vernon Edwin Neal

Christians in a .com World:
Getting Connected Without Being Consumed
by Gene Edward Veith, Jr. and Chris Stamper

Called to Womanhood:
A Biblical View for Today's World
by Beth Impson

God at Work:
Your Christian Vocation in All of Life
by Gene Edward Veith, Jr.

FOCAL POINT SERIES

Gene Edward Veith, Jr., general editor

God at Work

Your Christian Vocation in All of Life

Gene Edward Veith, Jr.

CROSSWAY BOOKS
WHEATON, ILLINOIS

Cover design: David LaPlaca

Cover photo: PhotoDisc™

First printing, 2002

Printed in the United States of America

Library of Congress Cataloging-in-Publication Data
Veith, Gene Edward, 1951–
    God at work : your Christian vocation in all of life / Gene Edward Veith, Jr.
      p. cm. — (Focal point series)
    Includes biographical references and indexes.
    ISBN 13: 978-1-58134-403-5
    ISBN 10: 1-58134-403-1 (alk. paper)
    1. Vocation—Lutheran Church. I. Title. II. Series.
BV4740 .V43   2002
248.4—dc21   2001007330

VP		18	17	16	15	14	13	12	11	10	09
20	19	18	17	16	15	14	13	12	11	10	9

To

George Strieter

Contents

Preface and Acknowledgments

This book is dedicated to George Strieter, who first introduced me to the paradigm-shaking implications of the doctrine of vocation. This he did by starting his own publishing company, Ballast Press, to reprint a classic piece of scholarship and theological reflection that, unaccountably, had gone out of print: Gustaf Wingren's *Luther on Vocation*.

George's own vocation is that of a roofing contractor, but his voracious reading and his zeal for Lutheran theology led him to start this other enterprise to make this and other spiritual classics available again.

When he gave me his reprint of Wingren's book, it sat on my read-someday pile for months. I had assumed that I knew what the doctrine of vocation was; that, yes, one can do every occupation to the glory of God. I assumed from the unassuming title that this just collected what Luther said on that subject. But both Luther and Wingren said so much more. For Luther, vocation, as with everything else in his theology, is not so much a matter of what *we* do; rather, it is a matter of what *God* does in and through us. And Wingren, a twentieth-century Swedish theologian, does more than quote Luther; rather, he systematizes Luther's insights in a sophisticated way and applies them in the context of contemporary thought.

Wingren's *Luther on Vocation* turned out to be one of those books that opened my eyes to things I had never seen before, helping me see my Christian life in a completely different way. I had a similar sense of illumination when I read C. S. Lewis's *Mere Christianity*. Keats had it when he first read Chapman's translation of Homer, that sense he describes in his sonnet of staring, astonished, at a previously undiscovered world. Wingren's book is a complex, specialized theological treatise, somewhat heavy-going for those of us who do not have a theological or pastoral vocation. (It is very much worth reading, though. Order it from Ballast Press at 1-800-335-4672.) My book sets forth what I learned from Wingren and Luther in much simpler (and arguably sometimes oversimplified) terms for laypeople like myself. After all, it is we laypeople who most need to understand the nature of our callings in the world.

The debt this book owes to Wingren is obvious and hereby acknowledged. But just as the Pacific Ocean existed before the conquistadors in Keats's poem discovered it, the doctrine of vocation has been an important part of Reformation spirituality for centuries. In studying this concept further, I was helped not only by other writings on the subject but by a number of pastors who have been teaching these truths to their flocks throughout their ministries. I should mention particularly Rev. John Pless, Rev. Mark Sell, and Rev. Steven Hein, whose insights have helped me sharpen my understanding of this doctrine.

In the meantime, the place where I have been called to teach, Concordia University-Wisconsin, whose visionary President Dr. Patrick Ferry is strongly committed to the doctrine of vocation, instituted the Cranach Institute, named after Luther's friend the artist, to study, apply, and promote the idea of vocation. As its director, I want to acknowledge the board members, pastors, and laypeople who "get" the idea and who have helped me greatly in this venture: George Strieter (again), Bruce Gee, Ilona Kuchta, Rev. Todd Peperkorn, and Rev. David Speers (who, I understand, introduced George to Wingren's book).

Thanks too to those I am privileged to know so well in my vocation within the family: My wife Jackquelyn and my now grown children, Paul, Joanna, and Mary, whose own vocational struggles greatly helped me to think through these issues as they apply in the real world.

CHAPTER ONE

Introduction:
The Christian's Calling in the World

🌀

When we pray the Lord's Prayer, observed Luther, we ask God to give us this day our daily bread. And He does give us our daily bread. He does it by means of the farmer who planted and harvested the grain, the baker who made the flour into bread, the person who prepared our meal. We might today add the truck drivers who hauled the produce, the factory workers in the food processing plant, the warehouse men, the wholesale distributors, the stock boys, the lady at the checkout counter. Also playing their part are the bankers, futures investors, advertisers, lawyers, agricultural scientists, mechanical engineers, and every other player in the nation's economic system. All of these were instrumental in enabling you to eat your morning bagel.

Before you ate, you probably gave thanks to God for your food, as is fitting. He is caring for your physical needs, as with every other kind of need you have, preserving your life through His gifts. "He provides food for those who fear him" (Psalm

111:5); also to those who do not fear Him, "to all flesh" (136:25). And He does so by using other human beings. It is still God who is responsible for giving us our daily bread. Though He could give it to us directly, by a miraculous provision, as He once did for the children of Israel when He fed them daily with manna, God has chosen to work through human beings, who, in their different capacities and according to their different talents, serve each other. This is the doctrine of vocation.

To use another of Luther's examples, God could have decided to populate the earth by creating each new person from the dust, as He did Adam. Instead, He chose to create new life through the *vocation* of husbands and wives, fathers and mothers. God calls men and women together and grants them the unfathomable ability to have children. He calls people into families, in which—through the love and care of the parents—He extends His love and care for children. This is the doctrine of vocation.

When we or a loved one gets sick, we pray for healing. Certainly God can and sometimes does grant healing through a miracle. But normally He grants healing through the *vocations* of doctors, nurses, pharmacists, lab technicians, and the like. It is still God who heals us, but He works through the means of skilled, talented, divinely equipped human beings.

When God blesses us, He almost always does it through other people. The ability to read God's Word is an inexpressibly precious blessing, but reading is an ability that did not spring fully formed in our young minds. It required the *vocation* of teachers. God protects us through the cop on the beat and the whole panoply of the legal system. He gives us beauty and meaning through artists. He lets us travel through the ministry of auto workers, mechanics, road crews, and airline employees. He keeps us clean through the work of garbage collectors, plumbers, sanitation workers, and the sometimes undocumented aliens who clean our hotel rooms. He brings people to salvation through pastors and through anyone else who proclaims the Gospel of Jesus Christ to the lost. The fast-food worker, the inventor; the clerical assistant, the scientist; the accountant, the musician—they all have high callings, used by God to bless and serve His people and His creation.

Not that they always seem that way, from the point of view of the people in those vocations. It is easy to see how all of these kinds of work are blessings to the rest of us, who receive their benefits; but from the perspective of the people slaving away in these vocations, their work is often a daily grind, a hard, boring, thankless task. Those in any particular line of work are usually doing it not from some high ideal but because they have to make a living. There may be some professions that are innately satisfying, but even high-paid and high-status jobs can wear the spirit down. Work often appears meaningless. It is a means to an end—survival; but it seems that we survive only to work. It consumes our time, our emotions, our after-hours preoccupations. It takes away the time we would like to spend with our families—though the vocation of family life is often a frustrating struggle as well—and as current technology puts us on call twenty-four hours a day, seven days a week, our work consumes our lives.

Though work is a blessing, enjoyed even by Adam and Eve who were employed in the Garden of Eden "to work it and keep it" (Genesis 2:15), after the Fall we must labor in frustration and sweat: "Cursed is the ground because of you; in pain you shall eat of it all the days of your life; thorns and thistles it shall bring forth for you; and you shall eat the plants of the field. By the sweat of your face you shall eat bread, till you return to the ground" (3:17-19).

Though Christians believe that God is active in the world, and though a little reflection demonstrates that He is active in human vocations, it is also true that the Devil is active in the world. On paper things should go well, with people helping one another and promoting the goals of peace and happiness that everyone claims to seek; but sin spoils everything. Many people in the world do not get their daily bread. Many parents abuse—or abort—their children instead of caring for them. Many husbands and wives are at each other's throats instead of being the "one flesh" that God called them to in marriage. Many politicians exploit, deceive, and tyrannize their people instead of protecting their interests. There are cops who abuse their authority, teachers who do not teach, doctors who kill their patients instead of healing them, pastors who distort God's Word.

People sin in their vocations, and they sin against their vocations. And in not being aware of what their vocations are—and that there is a spiritual dimension to work, family, and involvement in society—they are plagued by a lack of purpose, confused as to what they should do and how they should live and who they are. At a time when, according to the polls, people's major preoccupations are work and family, there has never been a greater need to recover the Christian doctrine of vocation.

It is odd that such a liberating, life-enhancing doctrine has become all but forgotten in our time, passed over in our seminaries, sermons, and Bible classes. But the doctrine of vocation makes up an important part of the spiritual heritage that contemporary Christians have, unfortunately, cut themselves off from and are in such great need of recovering. It is more than an understanding of work, more than the slogan that we should do all things for the glory of God, more than a vague theological platitude. The teachings on the subject by the old Reformation theologians are remarkably specific and realistic, giving practical guidance for how this doctrine can be lived out in the real, fallen world. But more than that, the doctrine of vocation amounts to a comprehensive doctrine of the Christian life, having to do with faith and sanctification, grace and good works. It is a key to Christian ethics. It shows how Christians can influence their culture. It transfigures ordinary, everyday life with the presence of God.

VOCATION IN HISTORY

Today, in an age of unbelief, many of the old theological words remain, even after the faith that gave them meaning is gone. For example, people who know nothing of the authority of Scripture still use words like *inspiration* and *revelation*, applying them to a work of art or to a business idea. *Vision, mission, Spirit,* and even more technical terms such as *canon, hermeneutics,* and *synergism* are all examples of theological language drained of its original content and turned to more secular senses. *Vocation* also has a common meaning today. It has become just another term for job, as in "vocational training" or "vocational education." The term, though, is a theological word, reflecting a rich body of biblical teaching about work, family, society, and the Christian life.

The term *vocation* comes from the Latin word for "calling." The Scripture is full of passages that describe how we have been *called* to faith through the Gospel (e.g., 2 Thessalonians 2:14), how God *calls* us to a particular office or way of life (e.g., 1 Corinthians 1:1-2; 7:15-20). The doctrine of vocation is thoroughly biblical, as shall be seen; but, as with other scriptural teachings, it surfaced and was developed with its greatest rigor during the Reformation.

In the medieval church, having a vocation or having "a calling" referred exclusively to full-time church work. If a person felt a calling, this was a sign that he or she might "have a vocation," which meant becoming a priest, a monk, or a nun. The ordinary occupations of life—being a peasant farmer or kitchen maid, making tools or clothing, being a soldier or even king—were acknowledged as necessary but worldly. Such people could be saved, but they were mired in the world. To serve God fully, to live a life that is truly spiritual, required a full-time commitment. The "counsels of perfection" could be fulfilled only in the Holy Orders of the church, in which a man or woman could devote every day to prayer, contemplation, worship, and the service of God. Even marriage and parenthood—though recognized as good things, with marriage understood as as a sacrament from God—were seen as encumbrances to the religious life. "Having a vocation" meant, among other things, the willingness and the ability to live a celibate life.

The Reformation came about out of a conviction that the church had drifted away from the truths of God's Word, focusing on salvation through humanly invented works, as opposed to the Gospel of forgiveness through the work of Christ. In scrutinizing the existing ecclesiastical system in light of the Gospel and the Scriptures, the Reformers insisted that priests and nuns and monastics did not have a special claim to God's favor, but that laypeople too could live the Christian life to its fullest.

The Reformation notion of "the priesthood of all believers" by no means denigrated the pastoral office, as is often assumed, or taught that pastors or church workers were unnecessary, or taught that everybody could come up with their own theology for themselves. Rather, it taught that the pastoral office is a *vocation*, a calling from God with its own responsibilities, authority, and blessings. But it also taught that laypeople as well have *vocations*, callings of their own that entail holy responsibilities, authorities, and blessings of their own. Not all believers were pastors or church workers. They do not have to be in order to be perfect before God, a status attained through the blood of Christ; but all believers *are* priests. All believers, like the priests of the Old Testament, can come into the presence of God through the blood of the Lamb. All believers can handle holy things (such as the Bible, earlier denied to the laity). All can proclaim the Gospel to those who need its saving message. "The priesthood of all believers" means that all Christians enjoy the same access to Christ and are spiritually equal before Him.

"The priesthood of all believers" did not make everyone into church workers; rather, it turned every kind of work into a sacred calling. A major issue at the time was the prohibition of marriage for people in the religious orders. The Reformers looked at Scripture and insisted that marriage is ordained by God and that the family, far from being something less spiritual than the life of a hermit or anchorite, is the arena for some of the most important spiritual work. A father and a mother are "priests" to their children, not only taking care of their physical needs, but nourishing them in the faith. Every kind of work, including what had heretofore been looked down upon—the work of peasants and craftsmen—is an occasion for priesthood, for exercising a holy service to God and to one's neighbor.

The Reformation was accompanied by great social change. This was largely due to the expansion of education to all classes and walks of life. Again, this was part of the priesthood of all believers, the conviction that every Christian should be able to read the Word of God. That meant that it was imperative to teach every Christian to read. Before, this skill was in short supply even among the wealthy and the ruling classes. About the only people who could read in the Middle Ages were people in church work vocations. The bureaucrats and record-keepers necessary for government and business were, of course, also literate, and while laypeople could learn to read in church institutions, most of these functions were often performed by minor clergy—the word *clerk* comes from *cleric*. The Reformation churches, on the other hand, launched an ambitious general education program in an active effort to teach everyone—girls as well as boys, peasants as well as landowners—how to read God's Word.

Someone who has learned how to read the Bible can then take that skill and read just about anything. Interestingly, though, the schools started by the Reformation churches went beyond basic literacy and Bible reading. They implemented the classical "liberal" education, pioneered by the Greeks and Romans to equip a free citizen to develop all of his gifts (the term coming from *libera*, the Latin word for "freedom"). Though the Greeks and Romans had a separate, occupational education for slaves, the Reformation offered even the lower classes a classical Christian education that would prove "liberating" throughout the social order.

The Reformation, concerned primarily with the individual's relationship with God, bore fruit in the secular realm with social mobility, an economic boom, and eventually political freedoms. These were sparked not only by the new education, but also by the related teachings about the doctrine of vocation. Luther's "Small Catechism" with its "Table of Duties" placed vocation at the center of every layman's Christian instruction, just as his "Large Catechism" developed the doctrine in detail for pastors. Calvin and his followers likewise emphasized the Christian's vocation in the world, and the Puritans applied the doctrine with a diligence and intensity that would shape American culture.

The doctrine of vocation looms behind many of the Protestant influences on the culture, though these are often misunderstood. If Protestantism resulted in an increase in individualism, this was not because the theology turned the individual into the supreme authority. Rather, the doctrine of vocation encourages attention to each individual's uniqueness, talents, and personality. These are valued as gifts of God, who creates and equips each person in a different way for the calling He has in mind for that person's life. The doctrine of vocation undermines conformity, recognizes the unique value of every person, and celebrates human differences; but it sets these individuals into a community with other individuals, avoiding the privatizing, self-centered narcissism of secular individualism.

The Reformation may have resulted in a "Protestant work ethic," but this was not due to the pressure to prove one's election by worldly success, as certain social scientists ludicrously maintain. Rather, the work ethic emerged out of an understanding of the meaning of work and the satisfaction and fulfillment that come from ordinary human labor when seen through the light of the doctrine of vocation.

That the Reformation was the time in which the Protestant church enjoyed its greatest cultural influence—in art, literature, music, as well as in social institutions—also has to do with the doctrine of vocation. Recovering this doctrine may well open the way for contemporary Christians to influence their cultures once again.

THE PURPOSE FOR THIS BOOK

This book is an exposition of the doctrine of vocation and an attempt to apply that doctrine in a practical way to life in the twenty-first century. First, it will explore the nature of vocation—what is the purpose of vocation, how to find one's vocation, how God calls us to different tasks and how He is present in what we do in our everyday lives. Then the book will address specific vocations and specific problems common to them all.

According to the Reformers, each Christian has multiple vocations. We have callings in our work. We have callings in our families. We have callings as citizens in the larger society. And we have callings in the Church.

Each of these has become a major concern—and problem—for contemporary Christians. What does it mean to be a Christian businessman or a Christian artist or a Christian lawyer, scientist, construction worker, or whatever? How can I serve God in my work? And what if I don't have one of these fulfilling jobs? What about my dead-end job? And how can I know what God is calling me to, what my vocation is supposed to be? How can I know what I am supposed to do with my life?

And what does it mean to have a Christian family? How am I supposed to raise my kids? And what if I don't have kids? What if I am single—that state largely ignored by "family-oriented" church programs? What if I want to be married but can't find the right person? If I am married, how am I supposed to relate to my spouse? How are parents supposed to relate to their kids, and vice versa? What about all of these authority issues?

Should Christians become involved in politics? How can Christians function in a non-Christian or even anti-Christian culture? Should we take it over? Or let it take over us? Or abandon it? Do we always have to obey our rulers? How can Christians change things?

And what about the roles of pastors and laypeople in the Church? Who does what? Who submits to whom? How do church activities and responsibilities relate to our other activities and responsibilities? How do secular vocations relate to the work of, say, evangelism?

This book will address questions such as these. Not that it will in every case provide a straightforward answer to all of them, but it will provide a spiritual framework for thinking about such issues, and for acting upon them, perhaps, in a different way.

Unlike many books on how to succeed at work, how to succeed at family, and how to succeed at changing the world, this book will strive to be honest. The doctrine of vocation is utterly realistic, accounting for problems, sins, and confusions that beset each and every vocation. The Reformers had much to say about failing in vocation, about the times when our vocation seems to be bearing no fruit. What the Reformers say about "Bearing the Cross" in vocation, about the role of prayer in vocation and what it means to depend on God in desperate times, may be the most helpful and encouraging sections of the whole book.

I should say that this particular treatment of the topic is drawn mainly from Luther's understanding of vocation. Other theologians have written helpfully on the topic, from the Puritans to Os Guinness's recent book *The Call*. What is distinctive about Luther's approach is that instead of seeing vocation as a matter of what we should *do*—what we must *do* as a Christian worker or a Christian citizen or a Christian parent— Luther emphasizes what *God does* in and through our vocations. That is to say, for Luther, vocation is not just a matter of Law—though this is a part of vocation that neither Luther nor this book will neglect; rather, above all, vocation is a matter of Gospel, a manifestation of *God's* action, not our own. In this sense, vocation is not another burden placed upon us, something else to fail at, but a realm in which we can experience God's love and grace, both in the blessings we receive from others and in the way God is working through us despite our failures.

Luther goes so far as to say that vocation is a mask of God. That is, God hides Himself in the workplace, the family, the Church, and the seemingly secular society. To speak of God being hidden is a way of describing His presence, as when a child hiding in the room is *there*, just not seen. To realize that the mundane activities that take up most of our lives—going to work, taking the kids to soccer practice, picking up a few things at the store, going to church—are hiding-places for God can be a revelation in itself. Most people seek God in mystical experiences, spectacular miracles, and extraordinary acts they have to do. To find Him in vocation brings Him, literally, down to earth, makes us see how close He really is to us, and transfigures everyday life.

CHAPTER TWO

How God Works Through Human Beings

🌀

God healed me. I wasn't feeling well, so I went to the doctor. The nurse ran some tests, and the lab technicians identified the problem; so the doctor wrote me a prescription, I got it filled at the pharmacist, and in no time I was a lot better. But it was still God who healed me. He did it through the medical vocations.

God talked to me. The pastor was reading God's Word. In the sermon, he drew out of the Bible God's Law, which made me realize just how sinful I am; but then he proclaimed the Gospel, showing how Christ has done everything for my salvation and that I am forgiven in Him. I appreciate how God got through to me through the vocation of the pastor.

God fed me, not with manna but with what the teenager working at the fast-food joint gave me. *God clothed and sheltered me,* with the help of my employer. *God protected me,* though I wish the highway patrolman hadn't pulled me over. God *gave me pleasure,* thanks to the talents He gave that musician playing on my new CD.

All of this is to think in terms of vocation.

PROVIDENCE

This sort of talk seems strange today. We think of God in mystical terms, as an otherworldly magical power, not Someone so close to home. God works in mysterious ways, not in ordinary ways, we think. If He is going to heal us, we expect something spectacular—a miraculous rising from the wheelchair or hospital bed, something that doctors cannot explain. Sometimes this happens, but the usual way He heals us is more mundane, though nonetheless wonderful. If He is going to talk to us, we want at least an inner voice, if not a mystical vision. That He uses a Book—mere ink on paper—much less a preacher, whom we know is not that different from us, can seem like a letdown.

Our usual view of God today is that He is not part of the external world outside ourselves. He is either "far above" the everyday world or He is "inside us." The world, we assume, runs pretty much on its own. The truth is, God does indeed transcend His creation, but He also governs it. "He himself gives to all mankind life and breath and everything," says the apostle Paul. "He is not actually far from each one of us, for 'in him we live and move and have our being'" (Acts 17:25, 27-28).

Christians in the past have taken for granted the notion of God's "providence." Coming from the word "to provide," the term refers not just to God's control in a deterministic sense, but to God's *care* that He exercises over everything that exists.

One of the consequences of "modernity," that secularizing frame of mind that has been dominant in the culture from the Enlightenment to the last century, has been to drain any trace of God—even any trace of meaning—from the objective world. Science, it has been thought, fully accounts for everything in nature and society. Rational but impersonal natural laws explain everything that exists. Religion is fine, if someone needs it, but it is a wholly private matter, an inner, experiential, mystical set of feelings that might make a person feel better, but that can have no bearing on "the real world."

The existentialists of the latter part of the modern era, laying the groundwork for postmodernism, went further. The external world, they said, is, strictly speaking, meaningless. Yes, it follows natural laws, but these are only absurd repetitions, as meaningless, to use one existentialist's description, as a lunatic mouthing the same words over and over again. Meaning is a purely human creation. Though we live in a meaningless universe, human beings can create meanings for themselves—values, commitments, even religions—to enable them to survive with dignity in a meaningless world. It follows, of course, that meaning is private and such constructed "truths" are relative. One person's meaning is not valid for anyone else. It cannot claim the status of objective truth. Existentialists could allow for Christianity, as long as it was a Christianity that did not intrude itself upon anyone else or insist on truth claims about the objective universe. Religion was allowed as long as it stayed inside a person's mind. An objective God was ruled out, though a subjective deity, roughly equivalent to a divinized self, was socially acceptable.

Remarkably, Christians went along with this worldview. Even while many of them rejected the atheism of modernity, they cooperated in driving God underground. Faith became reduced to a subjective experience, and Christian morality became just a matter of personal behavior, rather than a social necessity. Christianity became, as Francis Schaeffer put it, an "upper-story" experience, compartmentalized away from everyday life. Christianity became more and more withdrawn from the world, as did Christians, who generally went about their worldly occupations but did not see them as being related to the jolt of transcendence they sought from their faith. Even the Church, being a physical institution, fell out of favor for many religious people, who reasoned that if the spiritual life is purely interior, there is no need for external institutions. In the words of country singer Tom T. Hall, all that is necessary is "me and Jesus," and even Jesus lives inside my head.

How did this happen? Why did the external world cease to be perceived as an arena for God and spiritual reality? Surely the claims of modernity were weak. How can a natural law be both rational and impersonal? Isn't rationality evidence of a mind, of a personality looming behind what we see? And what does it mean to say that life is meaningless? Isn't there order, design, and purpose in every stage of life, from conception to death? Isn't it rather the experience of meaninglessness that is subjective, coming from the anguished heart of a lost soul?

I suspect that one reason Christians capitulated so completely to the new God-forsaken vision of the universe is that, well before modernity, they had lost the understanding that God works through means. Before, it was assumed that God causes it to rain. Then the scientists of the Enlightenment presented data about air pressure, relative humidity, and cold fronts. *That's* what causes it to rain, they said; we don't need God to explain it. But knowing the chemical and meteorological processes involved by no means diminishes the fact that it is still God who makes it rain. He is the one who designed, created, and sustains all of these natural processes. He works through means.

The Christians of the Reformation understood this very well. Luther believed that God rules in two kingdoms: His spiritual kingdom, in which He brings sinners into the life of faith, in which He rules in their hearts and equips them for everlasting life; and His earthly kingdom, in which He rules everything that He created (that is to say, everything).

God's spiritual kingdom comes through what both Luther and Calvin called the means of grace. God does not just zap people into faith. Rather, He employs certain means by which He converts the lost and sustains His people. God's Word is the primary means of grace, the revelation of God in human language—vibrations in the air; marks on paper—in which the Holy Spirit is active, calling people to faith and nourishing their growth in the Christian life (Hebrews 4:12; Romans 10:17). God's grace, the message of His love and forgiveness through Christ, comes to people too through the Sacraments, which are tangible manifestations of the Gospel (the union with Christ's death and resurrection in baptism; Christ's gift of His body and blood for the forgiveness of our sins in the Lord's Supper).

God's spiritual kingdom finds tangible expression in the Church, in which His redeemed people gather around His Word and Sacraments. God employs this institution to give spiritual care for His children and to bring His saving message to others. This includes the vocation of the pastor, who has been "called" into ministry. When the pastor teaches God's Word, proclaims the Gospel, baptizes, and presides at the Lord's Supper, there is a sense in which it is really Christ who is teaching, evangelizing, baptizing, and presiding, working through the "earthen vessels" of the ministers whom He has called.

Just as God works through means in His spiritual kingdom, so the Reformers thought, He also works through means in His earthly kingdom. God works through the natural laws that He built into creation. He rules the nations, including those who do not know Him, by means of His moral law. And He works in the so-called secular world by means of vocation. That is, He institutes families, work, and organized societies, giving human beings particular parts to play in His vast design.

VOCATION IN THE BIBLE

The Bible gives a particularly direct discussion of how God works through the agency of human vocations in what the apostle Paul says about earthly rulers:

> *Let every person be subject to the governing authorities. For there is no authority except from God, and those that exist have been instituted by God. Therefore whoever resists the authorities resists what God has appointed, and those who resist will incur judgment. For rulers are not a terror to good conduct, but to bad. Would you have no fear of the one who is in authority? Then do what is good, and you will receive his approval, for he is God's servant for your good. But if you do wrong, be afraid, for he does not bear the sword in vain. For he is the servant of God, an avenger who carries out God's wrath on the wrongdoer. Therefore one must be in subjection, not only to avoid God's wrath but also for the sake of conscience. For the same reason you also pay taxes, for the authorities are ministers of God, attending to this very thing.*
> —ROMANS 13:1-6

The whole issue of the vocation of rulers—what their "subjects" owe them and the limits of their authority—will be discussed in the chapter on the vocation of citizenship. For now, notice how the Scripture says God is operative in human callings, even in officers who do not acknowledge Him.

First, "there is no authority" that God has not "instituted." This must include other nonpolitical and nonjudicial authorities as well—that of parents, employers (what the Bible calls "masters"), and other callings that involve one person supervising others, such as teachers, church leaders, and the like. The authorities "that exist have been instituted by God." Strictly speaking, God is the only true authority, the only One who holds intrinsic supremacy, the only One who has the right to command. Those called to be judges, magistrates, and other civil officials exercise an authority that has been lent to them, one that is not their own but God's. As one of these civil authorities, the centurion who came to Jesus, said, "I too am a man under authority, with soldiers under me" (Matthew 8:9). Civil officials are themselves under authority—ultimately that of God Himself—so that if they abuse their authority or transgress the authority of God, they are acting outside their calling. (As we shall see, the doctrine of vocation is not a formula for sanctifying the status quo; rather, it is a critical model that subjects the status quo to the Word of God.) At any rate, the pattern is established: God's authority finds expression in the authority borne in certain human vocations.

The Romans 13 passage goes further: Rulers are not only God's servants (again, placing them under the greater authority of God)—they are God's *instruments*. As the NIV translated it, they are the *"agent[s] of God's wrath"* against evildoers. That is to say, *God* punishes murderers, rapists, and other criminals *by means of* human vocations: police officers, judges, juries, jailers, even executioners (those who "bear the sword"). This whole passage has reference to those authorities who bring evildoers to justice, not to political leaders as such. In a sinful world, evil must be forcibly restrained or we would tear each other apart, making life on earth and any kind of social order impossible. Though we are all sinners and evil in our hearts, God restrains the evil we actually commit, by means of vocation.

This passage teaches another important point about vocation. In the text immediately preceding, St. Paul tells Christians not to take revenge:

> *Repay no one evil for evil, but give thought to do what is honorable in the sight of all. If possible, so far as it depends on you, live peaceably with all. Beloved, never avenge yourselves, but leave it to the wrath of God, for it is written, "Vengeance is mine, I will repay, says the Lord." To the contrary, "if your enemy is hungry, feed him; if he is thirsty, give him something to drink; for by so doing you will heap burning coals on his head." Do not be overcome by evil, but overcome evil with good.*
>
> —ROMANS 12:17-21

Then the very next sentence is, "Let every person be subject to the governing authorities," quoted above. First is the full-blown ethic of the Sermon on the Mount, teaching radical forgiveness and love even of one's enemies and evildoers. Then follows the seemingly harsher text in which the evildoers get punished after all.

Here is the principle (which will be discussed further in later chapters): What is permissible in one vocation is not necessarily permissible in another. In Romans 12, Christians are told not to punish evildoers. But this does not mean that evildoers will get off scot-free. God will punish them. "Never avenge yourselves," we are told; "'Vengeance is mine, I will repay,' says the Lord." We are not to take it upon ourselves to repay evil for evil; rather, we are to "leave it to the wrath of God." Whereupon the next passage develops the notion that the civil magistrate "is the servant of God, an avenger who carries out God's wrath on the wrongdoer." When we are wronged, our part is to forgive, overcome evil with good, and repay wrongdoing with kindness. It is God's part to punish our enemies, since His wrath alone can be fully just. This may occur only at the Last Judgment. Or, in the case of overt evildoing that destroys social peace and physically harms people, God will also avenge wrongdoing in the temporal plane, pouring out His wrath against evil through the vocation of the civil magistrate, who "carries out God's wrath."

Thus, when someone breaks into our car and steals our stereo, we are not to hunt down the culprit and shoot him dead. We do not have that authority. We do not have the vocation to do that. Rather, we are supposed to call the police. They do have the authority and the vocation to bring criminals to justice, and judges and jailers have the vocation to punish them. (More on this later.)

Other passages in the Bible support the notion that God works through human beings—indeed, that He is hidden in human vocations. God's fatherhood looms behind human fathers, the marriage relationship is a reflection of the relationship between Christ and the Church, service to one's master is service to Christ—these will be discussed later in the appropriate chapters.

Many Christians miss the point of these texts when they reduce them to "who has to obey whom." Though the passages deal with issues of authority and power, their subject is vocation, in the context of God's providence, which in turn means not so much control as care, how He *provides* for our needs. God uses civil magistrates to protect us. He uses fathers to take care of us, and spouses to bless us. As we shall see, each vocation, even the authoritative ones, also entails responsibilities for the well-being and care of those under its charge.

It should also be emphasized that God is working even through those who do not know Him. In His earthly kingdom, God is active in the secular sphere, even among nonbelievers. It has often been pointed out that the text in Romans refers to the legal system of pagan Rome, and other references St. Paul makes to the Emperor refer to the decadent, ungodly Nero. But though we often think of Rome in terms of a totalitarian state, the actual legal system devised by that great civilization was a remarkably just one, despite the cruelties of some of its administrators, and Roman law is the foundation for much of our legal system today. Still, it is apparent that God reigns even in pagan nations and works through those who do not know Him.

This point is made explicitly by the prophet Isaiah, who tells how God would use Cyrus of Persia as a scourge to punish His people:

> *Thus says the LORD to his anointed, to Cyrus, whose right hand I have grasped, to subdue nations before him and to loose the belts of kings, to open doors before him that gates may not be closed. . . . For the sake of my servant Jacob, and Israel my chosen, I call you by your name, I name you, though you do not know me. I am the LORD, and there is no other, besides me there is no God; I equip you, though you do not know me, that people may know, from the rising of the sun and from the west, that there is none besides me; I am the LORD, and there is no other. I form light and create darkness, I make well-being and create calamity, I am the LORD, who does all these things.*
>
> —ISAIAH 45:1, 4-7

Part of the problem with the apostate Israelites was that they had come to think of God as just another tribal deity, pretty much in their control. The true God is far bigger than they dreamed, and His sovereignty is such that the greatest earthly emperors are at His beck and call and, indeed, owe their position and achievements to having been called by God: "I call you by your name."

Theologians sometimes say that the term *vocation* ought to

be reserved for Christians. To be "called" into a particular work or position is surely a function of being "called" by the Gospel into a life of faith. While agreeing that God works through non-believers as well, they use other terms for their roles: *office*, *estate*, *station*. It is certainly true that a Christian, who understands his life in terms of God's calling, will look at the work placed before him in a completely different way than will a person, doing the same work, who is lost in his sins. I agree with the distinction, though for the purposes of this book, for the sake of simplicity and to minimize terms, I will use the term *vocation* to apply to both believers and unbelievers, though I will certainly discuss the differences between them.

It is important, though, to realize that God's power and His providential care extend beyond the Church, that He rules in the secular realm, even among those who are rebelling against Him. When He gave me my daily bread, did He use a Christian farmer? I have no idea. I would like to think so. (In the case of my daily bagel from a Jewish bakery, the particular people who baked it and sold it to me were most certainly not Christians.) It doesn't really matter when it comes to the efficacy of that bread to nourish my body. Though it matters greatly for their sake in God's spiritual kingdom, in His secular kingdom a Christian farmer or baker does not work that much differently than non-Christian ones. God's plans for the way crops grow, His design for biology, chemistry, and human nutrition, are the same for everyone. "He . . . supplies seed to the sower and bread for food" (2 Corinthians 9:10). He also sends rain to both just and unjust farmers (Matthew 5:45). The scope of God's power and care is far greater than we can imagine, and He is more intimately involved with all of His creatures than we can dream.

CHAPTER THREE

The Purpose of Vocation

ⓢ

It has always seemed odd that a religious movement, the Reformation, that denied that salvation has anything whatsoever to do with good works should nevertheless inspire a "work ethic" and a group of people, the Puritans, whose name has become synonymous with strict moral activism.

According to the Reformers and their understanding of the Gospel, we are saved sheerly by the grace of God, and we contribute absolutely nothing of our own actions to the work of Christ. In that mysterious exchange upon the cross, Jesus bore all of our sins, received all of the punishment that we deserve, and imputed to us all of His righteousness. We come to God as sinners, not as doers of good works, and what we receive from Him is pure, free, and unconditional forgiveness.

"For by grace you have been saved through faith. And this is not your own doing; it is the gift of God, not a result of works, so that no one may boast" (Ephesians 2:8-9). Though our relationship with God has nothing to do with our works, good or bad, and is, indeed, totally God's work, St. Paul continues, "For we are his workmanship, created in Christ Jesus for good works, which God prepared beforehand, that we should walk in them" (2:10). By virtue of our creation, our *purpose* in life is to do good works, which God Himself "prepared" for us to do. We are "[God's] workmanship," which means that God is at work in us to do the works He intends. In other words, we are back to the doctrine of vocation.

FAITH AND WORKS

Our relationship to God, then, has nothing to do with our works. Our relationships to other people, though, in the world God has placed us in, *do* involve our works. "In God's sight it is actually faith that makes a person holy," says Luther in his "Large Catechism"; "it alone serves God, while our works serve people" (406). As theologian Gustaf Wingren puts it, "God does not need our good works, but our neighbor does" (10).

Christians are citizens in both of God's kingdoms. In His spiritual kingdom, we rest in Christ; in His earthly kingdom, we serve our neighbors. The greatest commandments, as affirmed by Christ Himself, are thus fulfilled: "Love the Lord your God" and "Love your neighbor as yourself" (Mark 12:30-31). We love God because He first loved us (1 John 4:10, 19). Apart from Christ, we would know only God's wrath against our sin, but now, with Christ as our mediator and covered in His blood, we can know God as our loving Father. Now that we know God's love and are freed from the bondage of our sin, and now that Christ is at work in us to change our sinful lives, we can love our neighbors.

It is dangerous, according to the Reformers, to confuse these two realms. We dare not come before God trusting in all the good works we have done. This is the way of legalism and hypocrisy. We come before God as sinners. If we trust our works, congratulating ourselves on how good we are, we feel no need for Christ's forgiveness. But receiving Christ's forgiveness is the only way we can be saved.

This is why all vocations are equal before God. Pastors, monks, nuns, and popes are no holier than farmers, shopkeepers, dairy maids, or latrine diggers. In the spiritual kingdom, in a divine egalitarianism (which would also come to have cultural implications) peasants are equal to kings. All are sinful beings who have been loved and redeemed by Christ. In God's earthly kingdom, though, Christians do have different callings, and their complex relationships with each other become occasions to live out the love of God.

Again, Luther said that faith serves God, but works serve our neighbor. We often speak of "serving God," and this is a worthy goal, but strictly speaking, in the spiritual realm, it is God who serves us. "The Son of Man came not to be served, but to serve, and to give his life as a ransom for many" (Matthew 20:28). In our vocations, we are not serving God—we are serving other people. Luther excoriated the monastic hermits who claimed that they were doing such good works in spending all of their time in prayer and devotion. These are not good works at all, he said; who are they helping? To offer religious exercises as good works before God while hiding yourself away from other people who might need your help is to miss the point. Genuine good works have to actually help someone. In vocation, we are not doing good works for God—we are doing good works for our neighbor. This locates moral action in the real, messy world of everyday life, in the conflicts and responsibilities of the world—not in inner attitudes or abstract ideals, but in concrete interactions with other people.

The purpose of vocation is to love and serve one's neigh-

bor. This is the test, the criterion, and the guide for how to live out each and every vocation anyone can be called to: How does my calling serve my neighbor? Who are my neighbors in my particular vocation, and how can I serve them with the love of God?

GIVING AND RECEIVING

In God's design, each person is to love his or her neighbors and to serve them with the gifts appropriate to each vocation. This means that I serve you with my talents, and you serve me with your talents. The result is a divine division of labor in which everyone is constantly giving and receiving in a vast interchange, a unity of diverse people in a social order whose substance and energy is love.

I don't have to build my own house. Someone else builds it for me. Someone else has made my clothes. I depend on farmers, bakers, and grocery store workers for my daily bread. In exchange, I write books and articles and teach college students (a poor bargain, it seems to me, for what I receive).

Secularists see this as simply the economy, which it is, but theologically it is the interaction of vocations. Of course the farmer, a recurring hero of this book, does not love me as such. He doesn't even know me. But still, he is serving his neighbors in his vocation, and his work in feeding thousands of people he does not know is an act of love—if not his own, God's love working through him.

Just as in the spiritual kingdom our state is one of utter dependence on God, in the earthly kingdom our state is one of utter dependence on other people. This truth, of course, flies in the face of our contemporary values, especially for us Americans. We have an ideal of self-sufficiency. We would love to be able to grow our own food, build our own home, and need no one. Our horror of being dependent on someone or something else is so great that when we are sick, many of us would rather die than have to "depend on some machine to keep me alive." Many would rather be killed. "If I get really sick, I don't want to be a burden to my kids. Send for Dr. Kevorkian." Never mind that when your adult sons and daughters were babies, they were utterly dependent on *you* to feed them, clothe them, pay their medical bills, and change their diapers. Whether we want to accept it or not, self-sufficiency is an illusion. We *do* depend on other people—the farmer, the plumber who put in our water system, the doctor, our parents—for our very lives.

"It is not good that the man should be alone" (Genesis 2:18). From the beginning, God put us in families, tribes, societies. God ordained that we be in relationships. He ordained that we need each other. From ancient hunters and gatherers who had to join together to bring down a buffalo that is much stronger than any one of them, to the complex division of labor in modern industrial economies, we are all in this together.

But if it is true that we are supposed to be dependent on other people, it is also true that other people are supposed to be dependent on us. This is no passive, lazy, welfare-state dependence, but an active exchange: my gifts for yours; my vocation for your vocation. This is why St. Paul could make the seemingly harsh statement, "If anyone is not willing to work, let him not eat" (2 Thessalonians 3:10). The dependence of idleness is sharply rebuked (1 Thessalonians 4:12). The converted criminal is told not to steal anymore but to "labor, doing honest work with his own hands"—not to make him self-sufficient but "so that he may have something to share with anyone in need" (Ephesians 4:28), so that he will not just take anymore, but give.

In our life in the world, in the interplay of vocations, we are always receiving and we are always giving. This is the dynamic of love.

LOVE IN VOCATION

Since God, in the mystery of the Holy Trinity, is a relationship of persons that constitutes an absolute unity, it can be truly said that He is love (1 John 4:16), since love is a unity of diverse persons. This notion of love, grounded in the being of the Holy Trinity Himself, becomes the model for all relationships and all social orders. (Charles Williams, C. S. Lewis's friend, develops this notion, as does Dorothy L. Sayers.) God expresses His love as He provides for His created order, and He calls human beings into the process.

Though a world in which everyone loves one another may sound very desirable, the real world, we know, is not like that. There is surely more conflict than love. The farmer is likely motivated by the necessity to make a living, rather than by love. He knows no one else will take care of him, so he has to earn what he can. The clerk waiting on customers is probably not *loving* them. She cares nothing for them, just as they care nothing for her. It is just business.

Whatever God's plan might be, we live in a fallen world, in which even our work is cursed (Genesis 3:17-19). We are sinful, which means, as a rule, we are self-absorbed, not loving. And yet, for all of our sin, we nevertheless serve and help others even against our will—not of ourselves, but because of the power God exerts in our vocations. Wingren gives the example of what happens in marriage:

> The human being is self-willed, desiring that whatever happens shall be to his own advantage. When husband and wife,

in marriage, serve one another and their children, this is not due to the heart's spontaneous and undisturbed expression of love, every day and hour. Rather, in marriage as an institution something compels the husband's selfish desires to yield and likewise inhibits the ego-centricity of the wife's heart. At work in marriage is a power which compels self-giving to spouse and children. So it is the "station" itself which is the ethical agent, for it is God who is active through the law on earth. (6)

Perhaps a more dramatic example is when the couple become parents. Suddenly the husband and wife, whose self-absorption is tempered somewhat in their marriage, find themselves wholly concentrated on their baby, whom they serve wholeheartedly and for whom they sacrifice their own needs out of an intense and voluntary love. Their vocation of parenthood calls this love into being.

Or consider the ruthless owner of a big business, someone who cares nothing for his customers or his employees, but is only concerned for his own profits. He is sinful, lost, and subject to God's judgment. And yet despite himself he must keep producing goods or services that benefit his customers; otherwise he would never stay in business. He is also employing his workers, enabling them to make a living and to support their families. God uses him in his vocation despite his sin, for His own loving purposes.

For the Christian, love of neighbor becomes something consciously felt, as faith becomes active in love. Though we sin in and against our vocations, as shall be discussed, as we grow in Christ the everyday tasks set before us can be motivated and shaped by love.

The various vocations we have—in the workplace, the family, the society, and the church—will each be discussed in turn.

For now we must remember the purpose that animates them all. If the purpose of vocation is to love and serve our neighbors, it is worth asking, for each vocation, the question that the teacher of the Law asked Jesus: "Who is my neighbor?" "Who, in this relationship, am I called to love and serve?"

In the workplace, the neighbors may be the customers, who are to be loved and served. The boss is to love and serve the employees, his neighbors who are under his authority. They, in turn, are to love and serve him. Teachers love and serve their students; artists love and serve their audiences.

In the family, the wife's neighbor is her husband, and the husband's neighbor is his wife. That means that she is to love and serve her husband. At the same time, the husband is to love and serve his wife. The parents' neighbor is their children, whom they are to love and serve. The children, in turn, are to love and serve their parents.

In the government, rulers are to love and serve their neighbors, that is, their subjects. Subjects, in turn, are to love and serve their leaders. Citizens and rulers both are also to love and serve their fellow citizens, including those who are oppressed and the victims of crime or injustice.

In the church, pastors and laypeople, the congregation and the whole body of believers, are to love and serve each other.

These will each be unpacked in later chapters, but remember that the salient part of vocation is not so much authority as love and service. Those in authority over others, by virtue of their vocations, are obliged primarily to love and serve those for whom they have responsibility. There is no vocation that consists solely of being waited on hand and foot, receiving homage and obedience, with no corresponding duties to work for the well-being and happiness of those under the authority's care. This applies to parents, spouses, bosses, pastors, and kings.

CHRIST IN THE NEIGHBOR

God is hidden in vocation. It is also true that God is hidden in our neighbor.

In His account of the final judgment, Jesus surprises both the sheep and the goats with the revelation that they had dealings with Him when He was hungry, thirsty, a stranger, naked, sick, and in prison. It turns out, "as you did it to one of the least of these my brothers, you did it to me" (Matthew 25:40).

Thus, Christ is hidden in our neighbors, particularly those in need. What motivates Christians to love their neighbors is to see Christ in them. Particular neighbors may not be very lovable, but Christ loves them and died for them, and if they are fellow Christians He indwells them through the same Holy Spirit that we share with them. How could we not love them?

And this surely applies in vocation. The farmer and the others feeding the "hungry" are feeding Christ. The mother dressing her baby is clothing Christ. The nursing home attendant is taking care of Christ. Employers and employees, husbands and wives, rulers and subjects, pastors and laypeople, and whoever our neighbors are in our vocations—we are all to see Christ in one another.

He accepts what we do for others as if we had done it for Him. It turns out that when we love and serve our neighbors, we are loving and serving Him after all.

CHAPTER FOUR

Finding Your Vocations

§

So what is my vocation? How do I find one? Or, as the self-help books put it, how do I find the vocation that is right for me? Today children are asked, "What are you going to be when you grow up?" as soon as they can talk. College students are pressured into declaring a major on their application forms. Advice from books and consultants about choosing a career, going after that perfect job, and "vocational development" has become a big business in itself.

The Christian doctrine of vocation approaches these issues in a completely different way. Instead of "what job shall I choose?" the question becomes "what is God calling me to do?" Our vocation is not something we choose for ourselves. It is something to which we are called.

OUR MULTIPLE VOCATIONS

Our vocation is not one single occupation. As has been said, we have callings in different realms—the workplace, yes, but also the family, the society, and the church. Someone who is retired may no longer be in the workplace, but he may still pursue his callings as a grandfather, a concerned citizen, and perhaps as an elder in his church. Some people find their callings in spheres other than the workplace—a woman who refuses a job so she can devote herself to her children; the independently wealthy man who does not need to work, so he devotes himself as a citizen to philanthropy; the elderly shut-in who devotes her energy, as a Christian, to prayer.

Furthermore, a person may hold multiple vocations within each type of vocation. In the family, a woman may have a calling to be a wife, which is a task in itself, but she may also have a calling to be a mother, a vocation that involves different tasks in a different kind of relationship. She may also be a daughter to *her* mother, a vocation that does not end with adulthood, but only when that parent dies. She might become a grandmother to her daughter's children. Then there is her relationship with her brothers and sisters, the whole extended family. These are all holy callings and gifts of God.

In the workplace, a mid-level executive or a shop foreman might be a "master" to those he is supervising. At the very same time, he may be a "servant" to *his* supervisor. Both of these relationships entail different duties and kinds of service. Even the C.E.O. of the company, the top boss, the "master" of all of his employees, very likely is also a "servant" to the Board of Directors or the stockholders.

In the social order of government, a civil official may exercise a great deal of authority, to which the rest of us citizens must submit. But then the official comes up for reelection, whereupon he has to submit to us citizens. In a democratic republic, a citizen is not only a subject but the ultimate ruler.

Different church bodies have different polities, but usually a congregation offers a wide range of opportunities for service—

singing in the choir, handing out bulletins, maintaining the property, serving on committees, teaching Sunday school— which seem so small, and yet which prove to be enormous blessings to the whole community.

Another aspect of our multiple vocations is that callings change. A young man working his way through college may get a job in a fast-food restaurant. For the time being, that's his vocation, and he is to love and serve his customers and his shift manager by flipping hamburgers. If he is fortunate enough to be going to college, he also has the vocation of being a student, which has specific obligations of its own (study!). Eventually he may get that computer degree, and he may go into his lifework. That will be his vocation then. And if his dot.com company goes bankrupt, and he goes from vast wealth back to flipping burgers, he has a new vocation. At every stage his calling is not something that will wait until he graduates, or even until he gets that big promotion. Vocation is in the here and now.

And whatever our vocation is, and in the very way it changes—whether the course of one's lifework goes from poverty to wealth or wealth to poverty—our callings are not completely under our control; rather, they come from the Lord's hand.

> *The* LORD *makes poor and makes rich; he brings low and he exalts. He raises up the poor from the dust; he lifts the needy from the ash heap to make them sit with princes and inherit a seat of honor. For the pillars of the earth are the* LORD's, *and on them he has set the world.*
>
> —1 SAMUEL 2:7-8

Though the world has its ways, its status games and career ladders, with good jobs and bad jobs, great wealth and the minimum wage, to the Lord all vocations are equal in status. The person blessed with wealth dare not feel superior to others or look down upon those who have less. The exalted have their own responsibilities and unique capacities for love and service to their neighbors. Those with less have their own honor from God. And sometimes He delights to have them trade places.

YOU HAVE NO CHOICE

One aspect of the doctrine of vocation flies in the face of every self-help book and occupational seminar, every conversation about "your plans," and every agonizing bout of decision-making. Despite what our culture leads us to believe, *vocation is not self-chosen.* That is to say, we do not *choose* our vocations. We are *called* to them. There is a big difference.

This is clear in our primary vocation within the family that God used to bring us into the world. We did not choose our parents. We did not pick our brothers and sisters. Nor did our parents, really, choose us. They may have chosen to have us—or, for those of us who have been adopted, they picked us out—but they did not choose exactly how we turned out. (I suspect that even if the prospect of "designer babies" through genetic engineering becomes a reality, parents will still find their children's personality maddeningly beyond their control.) In marriage, a couple may indeed "decide" to get married, but it is not just a matter of "choosing" a spouse, a particular selection from a wide range of options. It is more a matter of being chosen—he chose her, but she also chose him—that is to say, being called.

Nor did we choose what country we were born in. Yes, it is possible to emigrate, to change one's citizenship, but still one's society, one's identity-shaping culture, is more of a "given."

Nor is our vocation in the church merely a matter of our

choice. Many people feel that "being born into" a particular church body is less authentic than choosing a theology for oneself. But as Samuel Johnson commented, the church you were raised in was the church in which God placed you. Certainly Christians should join some other church if they no longer believe what that church teaches or come to believe that another theological tradition is more faithful to the Word of God. But the "church-shopping" mentality can be dangerous, reducing membership in a particular manifestation of the Body of Christ to a matter of consumer preference, in which we expect a community of faith to conform to our desires. On the deeper level, whatever one's theology teaches about the role of grace and free will in becoming a Christian, it is evident that conversion is not a matter of mere willpower alone. "But to all who did receive him, who believed in his name, he gave the right to become children of God, who were born not of blood, nor of the will of the flesh nor of the will of man, but of God" (John 1:12-13). Rather, Scripture speaks about how people are "called" into faith. "Those whom he called he also justified" (Romans 8:30).

When it comes to our employment, though, surely we choose our line of work. When we were little children, people were always asking us, "What do you want to be when you grow up?" Even back then, we thought long and hard about what we "wanted" to be, picking at one time "fireman" and another time "veterinarian." In high school we were given information sheets on various occupations, giving the salary range and the employment prospects, to help us make informed decisions about our careers. In college, as early as filling out the application to get in, we were asked to choose our major and to launch off on the career path of our choice.

Despite all of this, it is simply not true, in the ultimate sense, that we choose our lifework. If I were to choose what I really wanted to do, I might pick something like "Major League baseball player." But no matter how much I might yearn to go into that line of work, no matter how hard I "choose" it, I could never get on a Major League roster. I do not have the talent or the ability. No matter how much I want to, I cannot hit, throw, run, or catch. No team would draft me. Baseball is clearly not my vocation.

When I was young, I really liked airplanes. So after going through the school career education materials, I started answering the question, "What do you want to be?" by saying, "An aeronautical engineer." I learned, though, that this involved more than making model airplanes. I was not good at math, and physics made my eyes glaze over. There was no way I could go into that career choice.

"What do you want to be?" is indeed a good question. But what you are is in many ways a given. Even your wants—your desires, your dreams, your choices—are a function of who you are.

That is to say, God—making use of your family and your culture—created you as you are. The doctrine of vocation has to do with the mystery of individuality, how God creates each human being to be different from all of the rest and gives each a unique calling in every stage of life. Thus you have particular talents, which you are to understand are His gifts. You have a particular personality, with interests, likes, and dislikes that not everyone shares. Such is the plenitude of God's creation that no two people—or snowflakes or leaves or anything God has made—are exactly alike. Vocations are likewise unique, with no two people taking up exactly the same space in the family, the nation, the church, or the workplace. Finding your vocation, then, has to do, in part, with finding your God-given talents (what you can do) and your God-given personality (what fits the person you are).

A college student might choose to major in accounting because he has read that accountants are in high demand and make lots of money. If he is not good in math, though, he will probably flunk his accounting courses—a sure sign that this is not his vocation. Or perhaps he is good enough in math to pass them, and even to pass his CPA exam. If he hates the work, though, if he is bored and miserable balancing books, he is unlikely to be a good accountant. This is probably not his calling.

A fellow college professor told me about one of his former students who just could not keep his grades up. He was dedicated and determined, though, so he kept enrolling in classes, retaking those he failed and studying night and day. Finally, exhausted, he realized he had to take a semester off. He took a job, for the time being, doing what he really enjoyed—namely, working on cars. As an auto mechanic, he found himself rising in the ranks at the garage, taking on more responsibilities, and earning more and more money. He felt that he should go back to school, but he could not bring himself to quit his mechanic job. He was apologetic to his professor, but he should not have been. He had found his vocation.

In our choice-mad culture, people exalt willpower to the point that they even imagine that they "choose their own values." When it comes to getting an abortion or having a baby, staying alive or being killed by one's doctor, either action is considered moral as long as there is a "choice." People choose their own beliefs. And whatever one "chooses" is right "for that person." Attempts to persuade someone of a better course or of some absolute truth are resented as an imposition of your choice, your will, on another person ("you don't have the right to impose your view on anyone else"). But the basis for intellectual belief is the intellect, not the will. Morality has to do with moral absolutes, not human desires. Christians know too that the will is fallen, making it a poor guide.

This is not to say that we do not make choices. Even in finding vocation, there are many agonizing decisions to be made, from what to major in to which job offer should be accepted (as well as other vocational choices, such as: "Should I join this church?" "Who should I vote for?" "Should I marry him?"). But ultimately, looking back, it becomes clear that our choices were themselves part of the overarching design of God. "The heart of a man plans his way," says Solomon, "but the LORD establishes his steps" (Proverbs 16:9). We *are* to plan in the here and now, but we can do so in the confidence that the Lord is acting in our lives and in our circumstances, calling us to His purpose.

OUT OF OUR CONTROL

Vocation is, in part, a function of the particular gifts God has given us; but we cannot know our vocation purely by looking inside ourselves. Our choices are constrained by givens that are outside our control. Neither are circumstances completely under our control. God, though, is in control of them all. While nonbelievers are trapped in their random, meaningless worlds, Christians have the confidence that "all things work together for good, for those who are called according to his purpose" (Romans 8:28). Notice that this promise is tied to vocation (being "called") and to God's purpose, not our own.

When someone calls us—even over the phone—we know that is no inner voice, but the voice of another person who is summoning us and demanding our attention. Vocation comes from the outside, having to do with opportunities and circumstances, doors opening and slamming in our face. Since God works through means, He often extends His call through other people, by means of their vocations. *Our calling comes from outside ourselves.*

Circumstances really are beyond our control, but they can lead us away from some vocations and into where God is calling us. I have had many students who had to drop out of college, even though they wanted to stay. Money problems, family emergencies, health reasons, getting married, or having children—various circumstances threw a monkey wrench into their career plans. Sometimes these could be worked through by just sitting out a semester or two, but some of those students never finished their degrees. They ended up doing other things, their lives taking a different path. One may lament the circumstances or try to change them or wait for a later opportunity, but in the long run, from the aspect of eternity, these developments can be seen as part of God's plan. These students did not go on the path they intended; rather, they were being called to something else, ending up where God wanted them to be.

Since God works through means, it is to be expected that He will call us through the instrumentality of other people, through their vocations. I may have the ability and inclinations for a particular job, but first I must be hired. My call may be received through an employer (the "masters" of Ephesians 6:5-9). If I cannot get a job in a particular field, at least not yet, that must not be my calling. Sometimes a person may have a choice, agonizing over which of several job offers to take, but that choice is not completely open, as if one could choose any job in the universe. Rather, first the applicant must be chosen. Whoever is authorized to do the hiring makes a decision based on the applicant's qualities and abilities. Then when the person accepts the job offer, and the contract is signed or the handshakes exchanged, he or she enters into a new sphere of responsibilities and service, a calling from Almighty God.

A person might want to become a lawyer, but if he or she cannot get accepted into a law school, this is not going to happen. Our vocations are, literally, in the hands of others—college admissions boards, medical school selection committees, employment agencies, bureaucratic hierarchies, or the person we love who may or may not choose to marry us.

Again, though our desires and inclinations are part of what constitutes our personality and can be what shapes us for our callings, it must be emphasized that our inner feelings do not entitle us to any specific calling. "I want to be a policeman" does not mean "I am a policeman"; no arrest powers will be entailed until the person is accepted for police academy, passes the requirements, and is sworn in. Nor does "I want to be a policeman" mean "you have to let me into the academy."

A major controversy in the church today is whether or not a woman can serve in the office of the pastoral ministry. Being the pastor of a congregation is indeed a special calling from God, as will be discussed. Different denominations, of course, have different polities and different understandings and requirements of the pastoral office, with some allowing women to be pastors and others not. But a common fallacy in the debate has to do with confusion about where the calling comes from. Some women maintain that they should be made pastors because they have a calling from God. They have the spiritual gifts that a pastor needs. They have the desire to preach and to serve a congregation. Therefore, they sometimes say, their church body needs to ordain them. If they do not, that body is setting up ecclesiastical rules against the calling of God.

But again, a calling comes from outside the self. In the church, pastors are called by congregations; that is, their divine call comes to them through the workings of the church as a whole, which selects them, trains them, and ordains them into the ministry. A woman who "feels called to the ministry" but who seeks to minister in a church that does not ordain women is in an impossible situation. She cannot be "called" to a church that does not call her.

Similarly, in our earthly vocations we must attend to how God is calling us through other people and through the ordinary circumstances of life. And we cannot assume that what God is calling us to is exactly what we want, though He has no doubt prepared us to be exactly what He needs for His greater purpose. It may not be anything glamorous either. Social status or earthly acclaim means nothing to God; so we cannot expect Him to care about that in whatever He might call us to. "He brings low and he exalts" (1 Samuel 2:7). Sometimes He might humble the hotshot, ambitious college boy to make him do the useful task of hauling garbage. Sometimes He might exalt an uneducated farm boy to become the wealthy owner of his own company. Though we must indeed work, plan, and scheme, ultimately, for whatever we have and whatever position we occupy, we remain utterly dependent on God.

VOCATION IN THE HERE AND NOW

Though we have been discussing "finding one's vocation," there is an important sense in which such a search is misleading. Not only do we not choose our vocation, but, strictly speaking, we do not find our vocation, as if it is something unknown, awaiting us in the future. Rather, our vocation is already here, where we are and what we are doing right now.

Certainly we may have different callings as we go through life, and we may be preparing for some future goal. But that must not be allowed to obscure the fact that the relationships, duties, and daily work that God has given to each of us *right now* is a divine and holy calling from the Lord.

A college student might be working for that M.B.A., but right now he is putting himself through college by working at a fast-food joint, taking orders over an intercom and shoving hamburgers at people through the drive-through window. That is his calling right now. God is using him to give daily bread to His people. He, in turn, is serving his neighbors through his work. Later he may have a different calling, one that pays better and that uses more of his talents, but for now this is his arena of daily service.

Being a student, of course, is also a calling. The duties of his office include studying, going to class, and finishing his assignments! The work he does for his professors and in conjunction with his fellow students is a vocation, which does not entail necessarily getting paid. The unemployed, the idle rich, and the retired can find ways of serving their neighbors. Those who do not have jobs are still members of a family. Even those without spouses or children generally have parents or siblings, if they are still alive, or at least cousins and other members of an extended family. They have a nation and a citizenship to which they have been called. If they are Christians, they have a church. The point here is not to identify vocations for people who think they do not have one, but to emphasize that our Christian calling is to be played out in whatever our daily life consists of.

If a person is married, *that* is his or her calling. Thinking *I should never have married that person* or *I have no vocation for marriage* is no excuse for divorce or abandonment. "If anyone lives in marriage, in a certain way of life, he has his vocation," wrote Luther. "When this is interfered with—by Satan, or neighbors, or family, or even by one's own weakness of mind—it ought not to yield or to be broken in spirit. Rather, if any difficulty impedes, let one call on the Lord. . . . For it is sure that here, in fidelity to vocation, God has insisted on hope and trust in his help" (*Exposition of Psalm 127*; quoted in Wingren, 195).

The difficulties in vocation will be treated later, but Christians need to realize that the present is the moment in which we are called to be faithful. We can do nothing about the past. The future is wholly in God's hands. *Now* is what we have. The future-oriented obsession of today's culture pushes our attention and our good works to the future, to what we are going to do later. We must "live in the hour that has come," says Wingren. "That is the same as living in faith, receptive to God, who is present now and has something he will do now" (214).

This means that vocation is played out not just in extraordinary acts—the great things we will do for the Lord, the great success we envision in our careers someday—but in the realm of the ordinary. Whatever we face in the often humdrum present— washing the dishes, buying groceries, going to work, driving the kids somewhere, hanging out with our friends—this is the realm into which we have been called and in which our faith bears fruit in love. We are to love our neighbors—that is, the people who are actually around us, as opposed to the abstract humanity of the theorists. These neighbors constitute the relationships that we are in right now, and our vocation is for God to serve them through us.

The doctrine of vocation, though it has to do with human work, is essentially about God's work and how God works in and through our lives. Finding our vocation is not just "finding my lifework," nor even "finding what God wants me to do."

Though these may be part of the vocational cross we have to struggle with, finding our vocation is largely a matter of finding where God is, the God who hides Himself in our neighbors, in ourselves, and in His world. Once we notice the Hidden God and realize how He is at work—in the workplace, families, the community, and the church—and when we realize the part we play in His design, we have found our vocation.

CHAPTER FIVE

Your Calling as a Worker

🌀

A Christian and a non-Christian may labor side by side in the same job, and on the surface they are doing exactly the same thing. But work that is done in faith has a different significance than work that is done in unbelief. The doctrine of vocation helps Christians see the ordinary labors of life to be charged with meaning. It also helps put their work into perspective, seeing that their work is not saving them, but that they are resting in the grace of God, who in turn works through their labors to love and serve their neighbors.

WORK IN THE BIBLE

God called Adam and Eve to work—and established vocations—at the outset of His creation:

> *So God created man in his own image, in the image of God he created him; male and female he created them. And God blessed them. And God said to them, "Be fruitful and multiply and fill the earth and subdue it and have dominion over the fish of the sea and over the birds of the heavens and over every living thing that moves on the earth."*
>
> —GENESIS 1:27-28

"Be fruitful and multiply" ordained the family. Recognizing that "it is not good that the man should be alone" and that he needed "a helper" (2:18), God ensured that he would be a social being, living in families and, later, in communities. Man was also given authority, the right to "have dominion" over nature. The command to "subdue" the earth and to work in the Garden of Eden ordained human labor.

Apparently human beings, having been made in God's image, were to work in a way that emulated God's work. The creation of the heavens and earth is described in terms of God's working. "And on the seventh day God finished his work that he had done, and he rested on the seventh day from all his work that he had done. So God blessed the seventh day and made it holy, because on it God rested from all his work that he had done in creation" (2:2-3). Later, in the Ten Commandments, God makes explicit the connection between what He did in creation and what He ordains human beings to do—to follow His pattern in both work and rest: "Six days you shall labor and do all your work [a command to work], but the seventh day is a Sabbath to the LORD your God. On it you shall not do any work. . . . For in six days the LORD made heaven and earth, the sea, and all that is in them, and he rested on the seventh day" (Exodus 20:9-11).

Thus human work is an imitation of God's work, a participation in God's creation and His creativity. Ruling, subduing, multiplying, causing plants to grow, making things—these are what God does, and yet God gives them as tasks to human beings.

But then came the Fall. One of the first consequences of Adam and Eve's disobedience was that God *called* them, but they hid (3:9-10). Then all of their callings, though remaining, were cursed.

God's design of the family remains, but its original harmony is spoiled by sin. Adam and Eve argue with each other.

Childbearing remains joyful, but it will also be painful. The woman will desire her husband, but she will be ruled by him (3:16). Their oldest son rebels to the point of killing his brother (4:1-16). Not only the family but citizenship, the calling to live in a larger society, becomes problematic, as civilization itself— though good—is described as having been founded by sinners: Cain the murderer builds the first city (4:17); his progeny Jabal founded the nomadic tribes (4:20); Jubal, "the father of all those who play the lyre and pipe," invented the arts (4:21); Tubal-cain, "the forger of all instruments of bronze and iron," invented technology (4:22).

Adam's work remained, and his commands to rule the earth and subdue it and to increase and multiply were not rescinded. But now he had to labor under a curse. Now the ground would only yield the food he and his family needed to live through painful toil. Now his work would produce not just food but "thorns and thistles." That is to say, his work would often be in vain, giving him what he did not want—frustrations and bleeding hands. His work, previously so easy and pleasant in the Garden of Eden, now would wear him out. He must work by the sweat of his brow (3:17-19).

This then is the human condition: Work is a blessing; work is a curse. Work can indeed be satisfying, since it is what we were made for, but it can also be frustrating, pointless, and exhausting. Work is a virtue, but it is tainted by sin.

With the curse, though, came the promise that the Seed of the woman would crush the Serpent under His feet (3:15), a prophecy of Mary's Son whose heel would be nailed to the cross, but who would thereby defeat Satan once and for all. In Christ, salvation does not depend on our work at all, but on His work, accomplished in His sinless life and atoning death on the cross. His work is imputed to us.

This means that when it comes to salvation, we do not have to work. We rest in Christ.

An important theme in what the Bible says about work has to do with the Sabbath. Under the Levitical law, people who insisted on working all the time, who refused to rest, were subject to the death penalty.

"Remember the Sabbath day, to keep it holy" is one of the Ten Commandments, right up there with not killing, stealing, or committing adultery. Of course, its main significance has to do with worshiping God, with attending to His Word, which alone, said Luther, can make something holy. But the Old Testament makes clear that the Sabbath's holiness is to be recognized by not working on that day.

Christians have often disagreed about how strictly to observe the Sabbath. Does this mean that all businesses should be shut down? Is shopping work? Does playing a game violate the Sabbath? How about watching sports on TV? Is it lawful to have fun on the Sabbath? It should be remembered that the Sabbath, properly speaking, is not just Law but Gospel. When Jesus was accused of breaking the Sabbath by helping people, He set forth an important principle: "The Sabbath was made for man, not man for the Sabbath" (Mark 2:27). That is to say, the Sabbath is God's gift to busy, distracted, weary human beings. He gives us a break, time to recharge our lives by spending time with Him, our families, and ourselves.

Above all, the Sabbath speaks to us of Christ. That God wants us to honor Him by not working is a reminder that we are not saved by our works, that in Christ we enjoy a Sabbath-rest: "There remains a Sabbath-rest for the people of God; for whoever has entered God's rest has also rested from his own works, as God did from his" (Hebrews 4:9-10).

Spiritually we rest; physically we work. Though we still have to work by the sweat of our brows, and though our work still may yield thorns and thistles, those who rest in God's grace can know that He, in His creative power and loving providence, is the One who looms behind the work that we do. As Gustaf Wingren puts it, first quoting Luther, "'He gives the wool, but not without our labor. If it is on the sheep, it makes no garment.' God gives the wool, but it must be sheared, carded, spun, etc. In these vocations God's creative work moves on, coming to its destination only with the neighbor who needs the clothing" (*Sermon of 1525*, Wingren, 8-9).

IN THE WORLD, BUT NOT OF THE WORLD

As we have said, God calls people to different kinds of labor as part of His governance of the world. God Himself is operative in human labor, through His providential power. Though human beings tend to be oblivious to the spiritual significance of the ordinary things they do, and though their work is tainted by sin, the Christian, walking by faith and resting in Christ, can live and work as a channel for the gifts of God. God does not treat our works or our vocation as meriting His favor; rather, our relationship with Him is solely based on His free grace and forgiveness through the work of Christ. Good works, which are primarily done within vocation, are the fruits of faith. Good works are done not for God but for the neighbor. The whole purpose of every vocation is to "love your neighbor as yourself" (Matthew 22:39).

It follows that not every occupation or way of making a living can be a vocation. Being a drug dealer is not a calling from God. This particular job does not involve loving one's neighbors; rather, it harms them. Occupations such as thief, embezzler, contract killer, and other crimes would also be outside the pale of vocation. They are intrinsically sinful. They show no love and service. God is not hidden in them. Only the Devil is.

Even some legal jobs are not legitimate vocations. An abortionist is not loving and serving his neighbor, the child in the womb; rather, he is killing his neighbor. Making or selling products that are legal but harmful is no vocation from God. Nor is making or selling products that do not benefit the neighbor—all of the legal scams, bogus medicines, and wastes of money that are on the market today. Being a member of the "idle rich" is no vocation, unless the wealth is used somehow, through productive investment or philanthropy, to be of benefit to someone else.

Many occupations, legal and well-paying, consist of leading people into sin. This is what the Devil does. It is not God but the Devil who is hidden in the work of the pornographer, the strip-club performer or operator, the casino tycoons. Those in the entertainment business—actors, filmmakers, musicians—enjoy a legitimate calling. Entertaining their neighbors, giving pleasure to them, and perhaps giving them insight (as good art always does) is a way of loving and serving them. But sometimes their directors push them to create the pleasure of sin in their audiences. Here the Christian in that vocation must draw the line. Being an actress may be a worthy vocation for a Christian, but doing a nude scene is no part of her divine calling. Musical talent is a remarkable gift from God, but playing in a Death Metal band that celebrates mayhem, sadism, and the occult can hardly be what God has in mind for the use of those gifts. Instead of corrupting their neighbors, Christian artists are called to serve them through their artistic gifts, which may create conflict with their nonbelieving colleagues. That is to say, like all Christians, they must battle the temptations of the world.

Christians are to be in the world, but not of the world. The way this is accomplished is through vocation. Christ's words are so important that they deserve to be quoted here:

> *I have given them your word, and the world has hated them because they are not of the world, just as I am not of the world. I do not ask that you take them out of the world, but that you keep them from the evil one. They are not of the world, just as I am not of the world. Sanctify them in the truth; your word is truth. As you sent me into the world, so I have sent them into the world.*
>
> —JOHN 17:14-18

Christians live in tension with the fallen world. And they are not allowed to eliminate the tension by either retreating from the world or by uncritically embracing it. They are not "of" the world; that is, they do not belong to it. They belong to Christ. Yet Christ does not want them taken out of the world. He wants us protected from the Devil, yet active in the world, which, after all, He made and over which He is ultimately sovereign. More than that, He *sends* His followers into the world. That is, He calls them into the world.

Christians are engaged in the world by carrying out their vocations. This is how they can be a positive influence in the culture. Christian actors, musicians, and artists can be salt and light in a realm that is often tasteless and dark. This is why we need Christians in law, politics, science, journalism, education, academia, and all the other culture-making professions.

Furthermore, it is in vocation that evangelism can most effectively happen. How can non-Christians be reached with the Gospel? By definition, they are unlikely to come to church. Perhaps an evangelist might knock on their doors, but these days they may never let him in. But in the workplace, non-Christians and Christians work together and get to know each other.

Occasions for witnessing and inviting a colleague to church come up in natural ways—over the watercooler or during a coffee break, discussing a disaster like the World Trade Center attack or a failing marriage, or in times of joy such as the birth of a child. Christians penetrating their world in vocations have access to more nonbelievers than a pastor does.

Christians will come from a different place, so to speak, and their work may have a different meaning for them; and yet, in most vocations, the work of a Christian and a non-Christian will be the same. There is no distinctly Christian way of being a carpenter or an actor or a musician. Christian and non-Christian factory workers, farmers, lawyers, and bankers do pretty much the same thing. Perhaps a Christian might be unusually honest or ethical, but honesty and ethical behavior is expected of the non-Christian worker as well. Remember, non-Christians too have been placed in their positions and are being used by the God they do not even know. Each vocation has its own purpose, and it is basically the same for Christians and non-Christians. A business executive must make a profit for the stockholders. A Christian office worker must not give away the company's money or put up with nonproductive employees. A Christian police officer must not forgive all of the criminals and never make any arrests. To do so would be a violation of one's vocation.

Spiritually the Christian's life is hidden with Christ in God (Colossians 3:3). But physically the Christian lives in the same world with everyone else, subject to the same natural laws, living in the same communities, dealing with the same sorts of practical concerns. Christians are not to retreat from the realm of the ordinary and the everyday; they are not supposed to be having mystical experiences all of the time, to be otherworldly, to the neglect of the real world in which God has placed them.

Many religions consider "the material world" to be evil or at least unspiritual; salvation lies in escaping the bonds of mundane experience through meditation or asceticism. Christianity, though, values the material world. God created it (not a demon, as in Hinduism) and "saw that it was good" (Genesis 1:10, 12, 18, 21, 25). Moreover, God entered this material world, becoming incarnate in Jesus Christ. He was born into a family, into a particular culture, where as the son of a carpenter He must have worked with His hands.

His disciples too came from different vocations. Many of them were fishermen; one was a tax-collector; the apostle Paul made tents. They probably fished, cut cloth, and sewed no differently from those who did not know Jesus, though Matthew the tax-collector, like Zacchaeus, must have become more honest in his dealings after coming to Christ. Sometimes the fishermen Peter, James, and John did have to leave their nets to follow Christ, though they returned to them soon enough after He died. After the Resurrection, they were called to the ministry of preaching and teaching. But they were not taken out of the world until they received their final calling to die, mostly as martyrs, and to then receive their inheritance of eternal life.

MASTERS AND SERVANTS

The Reformation theologians emphasized the equality of vocations before God. They lived, of course, in a hierarchical society with strict pecking orders—peasant, bourgeoisie, noble, king, emperor—and rigid class boundaries. In that time, choosing a vocation was largely moot. Your station in life was pretty much the same as your parents'. A shoemaker's son tended to be a shoemaker, just as a king's son tended to be a king. One might think that the doctrine of vocation would simply enshrine the status quo. Instead, it would eventually smash the class system, opening up a culture of unprecedented social mobility.

One reason had to do with the spiritual equality of every human being before God. To quote Gustaf Wingren, summarizing various texts from Luther:

> When anyone, be he emperor or craftsman, turns to God in faith, or, more concretely, in prayer, he is without the outer support which "station" gives in relation to others. . . . Each is alone before God. Before God the individual is as alone as if there were only God and he in heaven and earth. Before God not only does station vanish, but also every work stands as sinful and worthless. Therefore all those qualities are wiped out which differentiate among men on earth. But in heaven all are alike. There all simply receive, and receive alike, the grace of God. Thus equality in the heavenly kingdom depends only on the fact that it is the kingdom of Christ, ruled by a divine gift, the gospel, not law. (13)

On earth, though, distinctions and differences and various vocations are necessary. But they will all pass away.

While hierarchies exist in this world, even in our more egalitarian age, which still has bosses, employees, and organizational charts, it is also true that God does not regard them in the same way that we do. "God shows no partiality" (Acts 10:34). He is not impressed with social status. Wealth, possessions, position, and all other marks of prestige mean less than nothing to God, who delights to exalt the humble and send the rich empty away (Luke 1:52-53). For Him, the first shall be last and the last first (Mark 10:31). It is important to remember in understanding vocation that He does not operate as the world does, that He may call us to what the world and we ourselves might consider a position that is "beneath us," lacking the glamour and importance that we would like for ourselves.

And yet earthly vocations are part of the web of human relationships that exist in this world, and these include the exercise of authority and the obligation of obedience. Our nation is a democratic republic, but the companies born out of the free enterprise economy are anything but egalitarian. Their organizational charts show a hierarchy that would stagger the feudal system. Workers have bosses, but even the bosses have bosses, going all the way up to the C.E.O., who has to answer to the Board of Directors, who must answer to the stockholders. Nearly everyone in the workplace is like the centurion who came to Jesus: "Lord, I am not worthy to have you come under my roof, but only say the word, and my servant will be healed. For I too am a man under authority, with soldiers under me. And I say to this one, 'Go,' and he goes, and another, 'Come,' and he comes, and to my servant, 'Do this,' and he does it" (Matthew 8:8-9). What was notable about the centurion is that since he was "a man under authority," he could recognize the authority of Jesus. In addition, instead of just using his position to lord it over his subordinates, he cared deeply and personally about the welfare of the servant under him, to the point of asking Jesus to heal him. Jesus did, marveling at the centurion's faith.

The Bible speaks directly about earthly authorities, not only in the vocations of government, which will be discussed later, but in the relationship between master and servant in the workplace. (I quote here from the King James Version. The modern translations render "servant" as "slave," which, while reflecting the Greco-Roman division of labor, makes the text irrelevant to our times. But since all Scripture is profitable for our learning and since the Table of Duties in Luther's catechism applies this text "to servants, hired men, and employees," I believe that the principles are applicable across socioeconomic systems.)

> *Servants, be obedient to them that are your masters according to the flesh, with fear and trembling, in singleness of your heart, as unto Christ; not with eyeservice, as menpleasers; but as the servants of Christ, doing the will of God from the heart, with good will doing service, as to the Lord, and not to men.*
> —EPHESIANS 6:5-7

Servants (or employees) are to obey their masters (or bosses) as if they were working for Christ! Once again we see that Christ is hidden in vocation, in this case the workaday employer. Since authority, properly speaking, belongs to the Triune God alone, the authority earthly masters have must derive from Him. Servants of "masters according to the flesh"—a merely earthly order—are really "servants of Christ." All of the fealty that conventionally goes to the master goes instead, through the master, to God. The worker's obedience is not to the master but to Christ. He is not doing the master's will but "the will of God"; his service is to Christ. This indeed makes him an effective worker. He is sincere, dutiful, showing "good will," but he is not concerned about being a "menpleaser"; rather, he is using his work as a spiritual exercise.

This text is actually subversive of slavery, opening up a space for human dignity even in bondage and divorcing the allegiance away from the master "according to the flesh" to God. Later Christian nations would abolish slavery altogether, though the spiritual principles remain.

Further mitigating the often cruel working relationships of the ancient world, the passage goes on to spell out the duties of the masters in similar terms: "And, ye masters, do the same things unto them, forbearing threatening: knowing that your Master also is in heaven; neither is there respect of persons with him" (Ephesians 6:9, KJV). Masters are to treat the servants in the same way the servants were just told to treat the master. Does this mean that masters should see Christ hidden in their servants? Masters are not to threaten those under their authority. They are to remember that they too have a Master. If they mistreat their servants, they will be held accountable to their Master in heaven. They must realize that they too are under authority, the source of their own, but that He, unlike the social system, shows no partiality.

In the workplace, whether on a road crew or in a corporate office, the passage from Ephesians applies as Christians live out their vocations: Subordinates must do their work, as instructed by their superiors. In doing so, they find themselves serving Christ in serving their boss. Bosses, in turn, must make their employees do the work they are supposed to do, but in the way they treat them, they must remember their own accountability to Christ. Since a particular person may be both a master and a servant at the same time (exercising authority over certain subordinates, while answering to the next level of the corporate chart), both injunctions will apply every day.

In the exercise we began this book with, reflecting how God uses farmers to give us this day our daily bread, it is clearly evident how God works through human labor. According to Luther's famous saying, God Himself milks the cows through the vocation of the milkmaid (*Commentary on Genesis*, Wingren, 9). Ironically, it is sometimes easier to see how God provides through lowly occupations than through those with more status. It is easier to see how God blesses the world through farmers and milkmaids than through Madison Avenue advertising executives or Hollywood movie stars, though in the eyes of the world the latter are considered much better jobs.

Still, most lawful occupations do give service to others. If someone is willing to pay for a product or a service, they must consider themselves benefiting from it. Companies need advertisers to help them become successful, and Hollywood movie stars can offer innocent pleasures for millions. These are worthy vocations.

But no one should be ashamed of being called to a vocation through which God blesses people in more tangible ways: waiting on tables, digging foundations, hauling away garbage. Nor should those of us who are blessed by God through these vocations look down upon them.

As for those who work with their hands—on a shop floor, on a factory line, on a construction site—they are especially honored in the Bible, in a text that says much about vocation, ambition, and the Christian's life in the world: "Aspire to live quietly, and to mind your own affairs, and to work with your hands, as we instructed you, so that you may live properly before outsiders and be dependent on no one" (1 Thessalonians 4:11-12).

JUST DOING OUR JOBS

When the planes smashed into the World Trade Center, thousands of office workers rushed out of the building. Against the stream, police and firefighters were rushing *inside*. When the towers collapsed, hundreds of them, who had gone into the doomed buildings to rescue whoever they could, lost their lives. Afterwards the firefighters, police, and rescue workers worked round-the-clock in the wreckage, desperately trying to find someone alive, engaging in backbreaking, exhausting physical labor to find clues and recover the bodies.

Here is real heroism, everyone agreed. Professional athletes and movie stars, accustomed to adulation, said with one voice that they are nothing—those cops, firefighters, and other workers at Ground Zero are the heroes. Interestingly, when the heroes took a break long enough to be interviewed, they modestly put aside the praise. They said, "We are just doing our jobs."

That is the doctrine of vocation. Ordinary men and women expressing their love and service to their neighbor, "just doing our jobs."

CHAPTER SIX

Your Calling in the Family

The church was packed for the funeral of a lady in her upper eighties. She and her late husband had had a lot of children, and here they were, along with a whole slew of grandchildren and a passel of great-grandchildren. Add in the spouses of the various generations, plus nieces and nephews and *their* children, and the church was pretty much filled with family, all coming before God to thank Him for this woman's life and to commend her back to Him.

What if this woman had not happened to meet her husband, way back in the 1930s? What if they had not gotten married? Half of the people in the church, from the middle-aged grand-parents to the little kids squirming in the pews, would cease to exist. The union of that man and woman had consequences they could never have dreamed about, leading to untold numbers of new lives down through continuing new generations, untold numbers of baptisms, new marriages, and new children being born. Clearly God was working through this woman along with her husband in the family they started.

Every Christian—indeed, every human being—has been called by God into a family. Our very existence came about by means of our parents, who conceived us and brought us into the world. Again, God could have populated the earth by creating each new person separately from the dust; but instead He chose to bring forth and care for new life by means of the family.

The family is the most basic of all vocations, the one in which God's creative power and His providential care are most dramatically conveyed through human beings. Anthropologists point out that the family is the basic unit of every culture. The family, with its God-delegated authorities, is likewise the basis for every other human authority. Thus the vocation of citizenship has its foundation in the family, and the father's calling to provide for his children gives rise to his calling in the workplace. And even in the Church, the family is lifted up as an image for the intimate relationship that God has with His people: God is our Father in Heaven; the Church is the Bride of Christ.

We were born into a family, our very existence being due to a mother and a father. Being a child is a vocation, according to the Reformers, and we will always be the child to our parents. And it may be that we children, in turn, will be called into marriage—another lifetime relationship—and that we will be called to be parents, with children of our own. All of these are holy, divine vocations from the Lord.

THE MYSTERY OF MARRIAGE

"God sets the lonely in families," says the Psalmist (68:6, NIV). It was not good for the man to be alone, according to Genesis; so God made him a woman from his very flesh, instituted marriage, and commanded them to be fruitful and multiply (Genesis 1—2).

Marriage is a vocation from God. This was a major issue in the Reformation, which had to battle the notion that those who wished to be spiritual would have to take a vow of celibacy, promising never to marry or have children. Marshaling the biblical texts on marriage and the family, the Reformers insisted that there is no higher or holier calling than marriage, and that everything that accompanies marriage, including sexual relations, is a gift from God.

Indeed, Scripture makes clear that the intimacies and relationships of human marriage have profound spiritual significance. In some remarkable passages of Scripture, St. Paul describes the union of marriage as "a profound mystery," which speaks of Christ and the Church (Ephesians 5:32, NIV). At the end of time, according to Revelation, the Church will be revealed as the Bride of Christ, awaiting through tribulation the coming of her Bridegroom (Revelation 21:2, 9). The great love poem in the Bible, the Song of Solomon (or in some translations, Song of Songs), with its longing and its sensuality, is indeed about marriage. But it has always been taken also to speak of the relationship between Christ and the Church, or, expressed in more personal terms, Christ and the believer.

That is to say, Christ is hidden in marriage. Not that marriage is a sacrament as such, since even non-Christians get married. The Reformers insisted that a sacrament must have been established by Christ as a communication of the Gospel; so baptism and the Lord's Supper are the only sacraments. Marriage is a natural state, common to the whole human race, instituted by God at creation. It has to do with God's earthly kingdom and thus is licensed and regulated by civil laws. Marriage is not a sacrament but a vocation. Nevertheless, marriage is a tangible manifestation of the relationship between Christ and the

Church, though only *Christian* couples, through the eyes of faith, will be able to glimpse how this is so.

In the same passage that lifts up the marital union as "a profound mystery . . . about Christ and the church" (5:32, NIV), St. Paul writes about how husbands and wives are to treat each other.

> *Wives, submit to your own husbands, as to the Lord. For the husband is the head of the wife even as Christ is the head of the church, his body, and is himself its Savior. Now as the church submits to Christ, so also wives should submit in everything to their husbands.*
>
> —VV. 22-24

That is to say, the wife sees Christ hidden in her husband. She submits to him as the Church does to Christ. The husband, in turn, in his relationship with his wife does for her what Christ has done for the Church: "Husbands, love your wives, as Christ loved the church and gave himself up for her" (v. 25). The wife's vocation is to submit to her husband. The husband's vocation is to give himself up for his wife.

These passages are often construed narrowly as speaking of "who's the boss" in marriage. Indeed, they do speak of authority, but as we shall discuss, this is only a small part—and if taken as the only part, it completely misses the point—of vocation. The purpose of vocation, remember, is to love and serve the neighbor. In marriage, the wife's neighbor is her husband, and the husband's neighbor is his wife. The wife fulfills her calling by loving and serving her husband. And he fulfills his calling by loving and serving her.

The wife loves and serves through submission. The husband loves and serves through giving himself up. He is called to do for his wife what Christ did for the Church. And what was that? He denied Himself, took up His cross, and died for her. He gave Himself up, continues St. Paul, "that he might sanctify her, having cleansed her by the washing of water with the word, so that he might present the church to himself in splendor, without spot or wrinkle or any such thing, that she might be holy and blameless" (vv. 26-27).

This is no husband lording it over his battered spouse, no lazy slob in his Barcalounger demanding that his wife wait on him hand and foot. That is not the way Christ treated His Bride, the Church; this is not the way He treats us. The passage gives us a picture, rather, of a husband who sacrifices himself—his wants, his needs, his strength, his very life if it comes to that— for *the good of his wife*. Indeed, with all of the baptismal imagery and the feminine pronouns in this passage about Christ and His bride, the husband is to give himself up for her spiritual welfare. Someone who does that, by the same token, is much easier for the wife to submit to; great would be her trust, her faith, in a husband who loves her like that.

I would say too that just as Christ is the one who initiates our relationship with Him (our good works are the fruit, the natural response, to His love for us), it is up to the husband to take the lead in creating this kind of biblical marriage. This is not done by hitting the wife over the head with Ephesians 5:22, insisting angrily that she submit. Using the analogy of our relationship with Christ, it is evident that we can never be obedient through the Law alone, by just being told what we should do ("For if righteousness were gained through the law, Christ died for nothing!" [Galatians 2:21]). Obedience comes in response to the sacrifice of Christ. If marriage mirrors the relationship between Christ and the Church, with the husband in Christ's role, then the husband ought first to give himself up for the wife, whereupon in response the wife, playing the part of the Church, will respond by submitting to his good intentions for her.

The passage in Ephesians keeps going, saying even more about marriage, including the physical, sexual dimension:

> *In the same way husbands should love their wives as their own bodies. He who loves his wife loves himself. For no one ever hated his own flesh, but nourishes and cherishes it, just as Christ does the church, because we are members of his body. "Therefore a man shall leave his father and mother and hold fast to his wife, and the two shall become one flesh." This mystery is profound, and I am saying that it refers to Christ and the church. However, let each one of you love his wife as himself, and let the wife see that she respects her husband.*
>
> —EPHESIANS 5:28-33

Far from denigrating the body, as Christians are often accused of doing, the Bible affirms our physical nature. Moreover, this text speaks of Christ's unity with His people, not in vague "spiritual" terms, but in terms of the "body." The Church is the *Body* of Christ. Furthermore, Christ has given *His* body, broken on the cross, for His Church. In the ongoing institution of the Lord's Supper, He says, "This is my body, which is given for you" (Luke 22:19).

At the outset of creation when God established marriage (St. Paul is quoting Genesis 2:24), He ordained that the husband and wife become "one flesh." This is indeed "a profound mystery." The nature of Christ's unity with the Church, what it means that we are the Body of Christ on earth, and what it means that He gives us His body open up depths upon depths of theological inquiry. But it is here applied to marriage in a very down-to-earth way. A husband should love his wife just like he loves his own body. He should never mistreat or harm her any more than he would hurt himself physically. Nor does St. Paul draw away from the sexual implications of the mutual body that the man and woman share. Elsewhere he is even more explicit:

> *The husband should give to his wife her conjugal rights, and likewise the wife to her husband. For the wife does not have authority over her own body, but the husband does. Likewise the husband does not have authority over his own body, but the wife does. Do not deprive one another, except perhaps by agreement for a limited time, that you may devote yourselves to prayer; but then come together again, so that Satan may not tempt you because of your lack of self-control.*
>
> —1 CORINTHIANS 7:3-5

This passage is rather astonishing in how far it goes in affirming the sexual dimension of marriage. The husband and the wife are to satisfy each other sexually. Their bodies do not belong just to themselves but to the other person: The wife's body belongs to the husband, and the husband's body belongs to the wife. They should not "deprive one another" of sex except when both agree to devote themselves to prayer, but this should only be "for a limited time," and after that they should "come together again."

This sexual freedom within marriage is very different—and far more liberating—than today's secular attitudes toward sex. There is none of this "It's my body, and I can do with it what I want." No, it is not your body—it is your spouse's, and it is God's. There is certainly no sexual permissiveness here. Sex is to find full expression in marriage, lest Satan tempt the man and woman through their lack of self-control into infidelity or other kinds of sexual immorality. The point illustrates a principle about vocation that will be further discussed in a later chapter: Something may be good when done inside a vocation, but bad when it is done outside that vocation. Sex outside of marriage is wrong, but not because there is anything wrong with sex. Within the vocation of marriage, it is a great good. Outside the vocation of marriage, though, it is evil. You are not called to have sex with anyone other than your spouse. You have no authority to have this positive physical relationship with someone you are not married to.

There is good reason why there must be a vocation to have sex: By its nature and its purpose, sex leads to another vocation, that of parenthood.

THE MIRACLE OF PARENTHOOD

That the very creative power exhibited in Genesis—the capacity to make new life—is manifested in ordinary human beings who come together and have a baby is an incredible miracle. It happens so often that people tend to forget that it is astounding and that it is a miracle—except, usually, when it happens to them.

When a couple have a baby, the miraculous nature of what has happened is palpable. Though the mother and the father have conceived the child—which shares their DNA—it is, of course, God who has made the child through them. "You knitted me together in my mother's womb" (Psalm 139:13). God, the giver of life, is actually present and working in conception and pregnancy.

When babies are born, they are in a state of utter dependence. They cannot eat on their own, they cannot talk, they cannot even move around. They must be taken care of in their every need—washed, changed, fed, comforted. They depend utterly on their parents. This too is an image of the dependence we have on God, not just when we were young, but, really, always. Again, God cares for the child through the mother and the father, and the love they feel for their child is an image of the love of God.

Not only do parents—like God—bring the child into existence—they also—like God—sustain the life of the child. That is to say, parents are not so much being "like God" as God is operating in what they do. He is hidden in the vocation of the parents.

Moreover, parents—like God, or as vehicles of God—work to bring their children to faith. The great Christian poet Sir Edmund Spenser wrote in his marriage poem "Epithalamion" about how, in the conception of a child, an immortal soul comes into existence, a potential citizen of Heaven. It is the parents' job, or rather vocation, to "train up a child in the way he should go" (Proverbs 22:6) and to teach him or her the Word of God (Deuteronomy 4:9; 6:7). In churches that practice it, parents bring their children to baptism.

The Reformation catechisms assign the instruction of children in the truths of the faith not merely to pastors but to "the head of the family." The spiritual well-being of the child is to be nurtured not just in church but in the family, which indeed has the primary responsibility. This by no means diminishes the role of the church, whose Sunday school programs and catechism classes operate on the parents' behalf. Part of the way parents exercise their responsibility is to see that their children are raised in the church. But the family is something like a mini-church unto itself, with "the head of the family"—normally the father, though the vagueness of the term would give this vocation to the mother if she is raising her children alone—being a mini-pastor to the family flock.

To say that a parent is a sort of mini-pastor by no means implies the actual role of the pastoral office, though pastors of the congregation should remember that the parents have the primary authority over their children, and pastors should do nothing to undermine or contradict the parental office. (The only exception would be when it comes to the Gospel, when the call to follow Christ must take priority even over the ties of family [Luke 14:26]. Even here, though, the command to "honor your father and your mother" must not be broken (Exodus 20:12), even in the cases of unbelieving parents.)

When Scripture says, speaking of the commandments of God's Word, to "teach them diligently to your children," it goes on to specify that families should "talk of them when you sit in your house, and when you walk by the road, and when you lie down, and when you rise" (Deuteronomy 6:7). Family devotions, Bible reading, moral instruction, and—especially important—the mutual forgiveness of sins and the proclamation and application of the Gospel are part of the spiritual formation of children that happens in the family.

The magnitude of the parents' role, the remarkable power fathers and mothers have to create, nurture, and shape their children, both physically and spiritually, has to do with the fact that God is the true parent. Throughout the Bible, both in the Old Testament and the New, God reveals Himself as our "Father." Jesus, particularly, taught us to pray to "our Father who art in heaven." He is the source of our lives, our provider, our protector, our authority. What about children—in that commonplace affliction of our day—who do not have fathers in their lives? God promises to be their father directly, the "Father of the fatherless" (Psalm 68:5). That God chooses to exercise His Fatherhood through the earthen vessel of ordinary, distracted, mistake-prone men is another of His miracles.

THE VOCATION OF BEING A CHILD

Not everyone is called to be a parent, of course, but everyone *has* a parent. Being a child is also a holy calling, with a particular work and particular obligations. Even when we are still adults, as long as our parents are living, we are children to them, and this continues as a major part of our family vocation.

A baby does not have much to do—eating, sleeping, excreting, and being at the center of attention of Mom and Dad, who wait on him or her hand and foot. This is never enough, of course; so another thing babies do is cry.

Note how Augustine reflects upon his own infancy in his *Confessions.* First, in a close, precise application of the doctrine of vocation, he ascribes how he was nursed as a baby to the workings of God:

> But the consolations of your mercies (cf. Ps. 50:3; 93:19) upheld me, as I have heard from the parents of my flesh, him from whom and her in whom you formed me in time. For I do not remember. So I was welcomed by the consolations of human milk; but it was not my mother or my nurses who made any decision to fill their breasts, but you who through them gave me infant food, in accordance with your ordinance and the riches which are distributed deep in the natural order. You also granted me not to wish for more than you were giving, and to my nurses the desire to give me what you gave them. For by an impulse which you control their instinctive wish was to give me the milk which they had in abundance from you. For the good which came to me from them was a good for them; yet it was not from them but through them. Indeed all good things come from you, O God, and 'from my God is all my salvation' (2 Sam. 23:5). I became aware of this only later when you cried aloud to me through the gifts which you bestow both inwardly in mind and outwardly in body. (Book I, Chapter 6, pp. 6-7)

Augustine is not usually associated with the doctrine of vocation, but there can be no better analysis. The statement applies to the giving and receiving that is in every vocation: "For the good which came to me from them was a good for them; yet it was not from them but through them."

Though way too harsh, he paints a vivid picture of a baby's perception when he describes why he would always cry:

> Little by little I began to be aware where I was and wanted to manifest my wishes to those who could fulfil them as I could not. For my desires were internal; adults were external to me and had no means of entering into my soul. So I threw my limbs about and uttered sounds, signs resembling my wishes, the small number of signs of which I was capable but such signs as lay in my power to use: for there was no real resemblance. When I did not get my way, either because I was not understood or lest it be harmful to me, I used to be indignant with my seniors for their disobedience, and with free people who were not slaves to my interests; and I would revenge myself upon them by weeping. (Book I, Chapter 6, p. 7)

The indignation of a baby, the insistence on being the center of the universe and that the adults perform everything he demands, is, for Augustine, a sign of original sin, a babyish act of cosmic rebellion that lingers on even when we are adults.

Surely, though, what children do is part of their calling. Playing, for example, is what children do and, arguably, what they are supposed to do. Learning is part of the calling of childhood. Everything they do to grow up is part of their vocation, and it is the one vocation that everyone has had.

If childhood is a vocation, is God hidden here as well? Since God is our Heavenly Father, human beings are always children to Him. Yet, in the mystery of the Trinity God is Father, and He is also Son. Jesus Christ is Son of God and Son of man. In His incarnation, He was born as a baby, was subject to His mother and father, and perfectly fulfilled His Heavenly Father's will. Jesus Christ, begotten not made, is the divine Child, the model, the source, and the sanctifier of all childhood.

If childhood is a vocation, how is a child to love and serve his neighbor? Who is the child's neighbor? The answer is, the parents.

"Honor your father and your mother" (Exodus 20:12). The commandment is clear and binding, a moral principle on the order of not killing or not stealing. Luther puts it in a characteristically pungent way in his explanation of the commandment in the "Large Catechism." Children, he says, need to "realize that they have received their bodies and lives from their parents and have been nourished and nurtured by their parents when otherwise they would have perished a hundred times in their own filth," a reference to the obligation due to those who changed their diapers. "Those who look at the matter in this way and think about it will, without compulsion, give all honor to their parents and esteem them as the ones through whom God has given them everything good" (404).

Not that children might not still be embarrassed by their parents. Luther, ever-realistic, recognizes that parents will likely have failings:

> It must therefore be impressed on young people that they revere their parents as God's representatives, and to remember that, however lowly, poor, feeble, and eccentric[!] they may be, they are still their mother and father, given by God. They are not to be deprived of their honor because of their ways or failings. Therefore, we are not to think of their persons, whatever they may be, but of the will of God, who has created and ordained it so. (401)

However "eccentric" they may be! Luther here makes a distinction that is helpful in understanding all vocations, the difference between person and office.

Vocation is a matter of a person being called to a particular office. The authority, the prerogatives, and the divine presence belong to the office, not to the person who holds it. One's parents might be "lowly, poor, feeble, and eccentric," but they still hold the offices of mother and father. Not by virtue of their own abilities, but because of the creative power of sexuality in God's design of the human body, they became parents. By the same token, in other vocations a judge, for example, is an ordinary person with foibles and faults; but when acting in office, robed with the law and the authority of the state, the judge can exercise powers of life and death. The boss may be a jerk, but an employee must still follow directions. A pastor may be weak in the faith, but by virtue of his office the weddings he performs are still valid, as are, more importantly, his baptisms and evangelism. The person who holds the office is a sinner in need of God's grace and forgiveness, and though, as we shall see, it is possible to sin in and against vocation—as with parents who harm their children instead of loving them—the office itself is a gift of God.

The relationship between parents and offspring continues even after children grow up into adulthood. They are still sons and daughters. As long as their parents are living, those parents are to be honored. Discussing the treatment of widows in the church, St. Paul says that "if a widow has children or grandchildren, let them first learn to show godliness to their own household and to make some return to their parents, for this is pleasing in the sight of God" (1 Timothy 5:4). Many elderly men and women today recoil against being dependent on their children—sometimes calling for euthanasia rather than making themselves "burdens" on their children. But, again, dependence is what families are all about. Earlier their children—lying helplessly in their cribs, dirtying their diapers, and needing to be cleaned and fed—were utterly dependent on their parents. There may come a time when their parents become similarly dependent on them. Though the role reversals are traumatic for both sides, repaying their parents and grandparents are all part of the family vocation.

In this context, St. Paul goes on, giving a stern warning against abandoning the members of one's family when they are in need: "But if anyone does not provide for his relatives, and especially for members of his household, he has denied the faith and is worse than an unbeliever" (1 Timothy 5:8). Rejecting the family is equivalent to rejecting God, since He is in the family.

GOD'S PURPOSE FOR THE FAMILY VOCATIONS

The family is the foundational vocation. Other earthly authorities grow out of the authority exercised in the family. "For all other authority is derived and developed out of the authority of parents," says Luther in the "Large Catechism," relating parenthood to the other vocations. "Father by blood, father of a household [employees], and father of the nation [civic rulers]. In addition, there are also spiritual fathers [pastors]" (408).

Though authority within the family and the other vocations is very real, it is not the purpose of vocation. Many people immediately jump to issues of authority when they think of vocation, discussing what authority parents have over their children, what authority husbands have over their wives, then jumping to the other vocations to try to figure out what authority employers and civic rulers and pastors have over their charges. It is true that all legitimate authority derives from God, who is indeed present in these vocations. But to reduce these relationships to matters of obedience is to construe the doctrine of vocation as just Law when it is also a matter of Gospel. The essence and purpose of Christian vocation—from the point of view of the person holding the vocation and being a vehicle for God's action—is love and service.

In a well-functioning family, the parents are loving and serving their children. The children are loving and serving their parents. The wife loves and serves her husband. The husband loves and serves his wife. By the same token, employers and employees, rulers and subjects, pastors and congregation love and serve each other.

Since certain callings *have* authority, it is not usually necessary for those in those vocations to *demand* authority; there is no reason to demand what they already have. Their authority is real, whether they or their charges like it or not. What was said about wives and husbands is probably true also for parents and children, rulers and subjects: Acknowledging authority tends to come as a response to the love and service that have been received. Children will more readily obey parents whom they know love them; citizens will more readily obey rulers who have worked for the good of their people.

To be sure, we sin in our family vocations. After exalting the authority of parents—and that of other earthly rulers—in the "Large Catechism," Luther immediately calls them all to task: "Everyone acts as if God gave us children for our pleasure and amusement," he writes, "as if it were no concern of ours what they learn or how they live" (409). Authority entails obligation to those under our care. It is not just a matter of being served; it is a particular way of serving (cf. Matthew 20:25-28).

Parents were not called to their high office to neglect or spoil or be cruel to their children. God did not bless a man with a wife so he could dominate and misuse her. A woman was not called into motherhood to abort her child. Child abuse, mental cruelty, neglect, coldheartedness, domestic fighting, provoking children to wrath (Ephesians 6:4)—these have nothing to do with God's intentions for the family and are sins against vocation.

Parents are blessings to their children. Children are blessings to their parents. Husbands are blessings to their wives. Wives are blessings to their husbands. Even though the treasures of God's gifts are hidden in "earthen vessels" (2 Corinthians 4:7, KJV)—our own fallen and fallible flesh—He continues to pour out His love through human beings, whom He has placed in families.

CHAPTER SEVEN

Your Calling as a Citizen

⑤

When terrorists attacked America on September 11, 2001, a wave of patriotism resonated throughout the nation. Americans of all backgrounds and all religions felt a unity with their fellow citizens who had been so cruelly killed. The President called for national prayer. During the weeks after the attack, churches were full. Flags showed up all over the place. People started both singing and praying, "God bless America."

Was this wrong? Some Christians, while caught up in the positive feelings, felt uneasy. Should Christians be patriotic? Is so much flag-waving idolatrous? Though many felt that retaliation is surely justified against the enemies who attacked our country and killed so many innocent people, aren't Christians supposed to forgive? While the whole country rallied around the President and the military, some Christians were leery about these earthly authorities having the power of life and death. And some of the same Christians who rallied around President Bush had a hard time rallying around his predecessor.

Issues of church and state are hard to mesh, not only legally but in the Christian's personal life. To what extent are the two mutually supportive, and to what extent are they in conflict?

Some Christians have a guilty conscience about giving their allegiance to a secular state. We don't really live in a "Christian nation," they say, since only individuals can have faith. The "civil religion" of patriotism is not the same as saving faith. They worry about whether saluting the flag—or having the national flag displayed in church—is idolatry. They scrutinize their perhaps natural love of country as something to be wary of. Christians are to be strangers in a strange land, and if they are to be involved with their nation or their government, it must be as a critic, playing the role of the prophet denouncing the king.

But even criticizing the status quo and trying to make it better is problematic; if Christians can hardly keep God's Law, how can non-Christians obey it? Christians might believe, on the basis of their faith, that abortion is wrong, but how can they impose this position on people of other beliefs in a secular, pluralistic society? Other Christians insist that the United States *is* a Christian country, and if it is not, they need to make it one.

Again, the doctrine of vocation is helpful in sorting out the thorny issues of church and state. Being a citizen of a particular nation is a divine calling. God works through governments and is hidden in cultural institutions. As such, His moral law *is* binding, even among those who do not know Him, but in whom He still operates. The nation, though, is no substitute for and must not be confused with His Church. But Christians do have a vocation to be good citizens, in every way that implies. They are to see God's authority as looming behind the secular authorities who govern their nation. This includes obeying their rulers. In a democratic republic, however, the ultimate rulers are not officeholders but the people who elect them and to whom they are accountable. American Christians thus have the unusual vocation of being subjects and rulers at the same time.

FROM ALL NATIONS, TRIBES, AND PEOPLES

Christians live in the same communities as non-Christians. They not only typically work side-by-side with nonbelievers—they are citizens of the same nation. They have the same civic responsibilities as their non-Christian neighbors. Voting, getting involved in politics, agitating for causes, and trying to make their communities the best they can—all of these are part of the calling to be good citizens. Serving in the armed forces, pledging allegiance to the flag, loving one's country, and other exercises of citizenship are also part of the Christian's vocation.

I am presenting this from the point of view of an American, but this holds for other countries as well. Christians in other nations and in other cultures have a calling to be citizens where they are. The task is more difficult for Christians living in oppressive regimes, in nations that may persecute them for their faith. But even there they have a calling to be citizens.

Clearly, people are shaped by their cultures. The way a person thinks and acts, the family ties and social habits, a person's very identity is shaped by his or her culture. God uses social orders to form people according to His will. Though cultures are human creations, and thus tainted by sin to various degrees, it is evident that God works through them to restrain evil and to provide for the needs of His creatures.

God's moral law is built into human beings. "For when Gentiles, who do not have the law, by nature do what the law requires, they are a law to themselves, even though they do not have the law. They show that the work of the law is written on their hearts, while their conscience also bears witness, and their conflicting thoughts accuse or even excuse them" (Romans 2:14-15). The Gentiles, St. Paul is saying, do not have the fullness of God's Law revealed to them—for that, they need the Word of God, the Scriptures as delivered to the Jews; but they are still human beings. They have a moral sensibility "written on their hearts," so that they too struggle in their "conscience." They "by nature" sometimes do things that are morally right, since, after all, God's laws are built into His very creation.

Not that anyone can be righteous before God by keeping these natural laws. If they could keep them, that would be one thing, but no one does. The universal law of nature and of conscience merely renders all sinners with "no excuse" (Romans 2:1). Everyone, in all cultures, Gentile and Jew, needs the forgiveness made available through the Gospel. But the Law, operating even in societies that do not know the true God, is still operative.

The Reformers spoke of three uses of the Law: to curb the evil of sinners so human beings can exist together in societies without tearing each other apart (the "civil use"); to make people realize their sinfulness and to awaken them to the necessity of repentance and to their need for the Gospel (the "theological use"); and to guide Christians in living according to God's will (the "didactic use"). The civil use of the Law, then, applies to all cultures, Christian or not.

In today's climate of cultural relativism, it is often said that morality is just a matter of culture and that it varies from society to society. There are no moral absolutes, it is said, just different cultural practices. Well, the fact is, despite all of their differences, one of the few things cultures do agree on is objective morality. All genuine cultures have sexual taboos. All have laws against stealing and murder. All zealously guard what we would call "family values." C. S. Lewis, in *The Abolition of Man*, demonstrates the universality of the moral law, complete with a cross-cultural sampler of ethical principles. It is only our own Western postmodern culture that questions these ethical absolutes. True multiculturalism never would.

That our culture today doubts moral absolutes—or at least pretends to, since people are absolutist enough when it comes to their "rights"—is a reminder, though, that cultures often have embedded in them real sin, which it is the duty of its citizens to challenge. Infanticide, for example, has been the practice of the ancient Greeks, the modern Chinese, and advanced Western democracies that have legalized abortion. This is a great evil, no matter what the culture is, and no matter what other virtues the culture exemplifies. A good citizen of any of these societies would work to change such institutionalized evil, for the good of the culture itself.

In our own society, the attempt is often made to silence Christians, to keep them from acting on their moral convictions to address the evils of society. "Your religion tells you that abortion is wrong," they are told, "but other people have different religious beliefs about when life begins. You don't have the right to impose your religious beliefs on other people when it comes to abortion." But believing it is wrong to kill infants in the womb is not part of a Christian's *religious* belief as such. It is a moral, not a theological, principle. As such, it is applicable to all of society, for Christians and non-Christians alike.

What makes a person a Christian is not holding to a particular set of moral beliefs; rather, it is faith in Jesus Christ, which, indeed, can be imposed on no one. Being Christian is not a matter of behaving rightly; rather, it is a matter of being forgiven for behaving wrongly. Morality, though, is for everyone in every religion and every culture. Christians are right to work for social justice, to fight corruption, to defend the unborn, to crusade against pornography and sexual immorality. These are not religious issues as such, but moral issues. Christians in their vocations as citizens should uphold the civil use of the Law. Because they know this law more clearly, since they have not just a fallible conscience but the Word of God, they will tend to be moral activists. This is part of their vocation as Christian citizens. But they must not confuse their moral activism or political activism with their distinctly Christian spiritual calling to proclaim the Gospel to all nations.

Unlike most of the world's religions, Christianity is not a cultural religion. Islam and Hinduism are as much cultures as theologies, and to adopt one of these religions is to adopt a culture, complete with styles of clothing, types of food, and the social customs of Arabia or India. In contrast, Christianity is for *every* culture. This was affirmed in Christ's Great Commission, when He told His followers, "Go therefore and make disciples of all nations, baptizing them in the name of the Father and of the Son and of the Holy Spirit, teaching them to observe all that I have commanded you" (Matthew 28:19-20). This was evident when the Holy Spirit first came upon the church at Pentecost, and the message of the Gospel was immediately comprehensible to "Parthians and Medes and Elamites and residents of Mesopotamia, Judea and Cappadocia, Pontus and Asia, Phrygia and Pamphylia, Egypt and the parts of Libya belonging to Cyrene and visitors from Rome, both Jews and proselytes, Cretans and Arabians" (Acts 2:9-11). And in Heaven itself there will be "a great multitude that no one could number, from every nation, from all tribes and peoples and languages, standing before the throne before the Lamb" (Revelation 7:9).

Thus there can be Hispanic Christians, Chinese Christians, Nigerian Christians, Arab Christians, Christians from Korea and Japan and South Africa and Russia and Sweden and the various tribes in New Guinea—every nation and tribe. They are all citizens of the Kingdom of Christ, and they remain citizens of their own nations as well. God honors both.

THE VOCATIONS OF GOVERNMENT

God created human beings to live in relationship with others, to form societies and cultures. The Christian's involvement with and responsibility to the culture in which God has placed him is part of his calling. Human societies also require *governments*, formal laws, and governing authorities. Filling these offices of earthly authority is indeed a worthy vocation for the Christian, and the rest of us Christian citizens have a distinct biblical calling to obey them.

We have already looked at Romans 13, which spells out in detail—with implications for all of the vocations—how it is that God is hidden in secular government (see Chapter 2 of this book). It will be helpful to review that Scripture in this context:

Let every person be subject to the governing authorities. For there is no authority except from God, and those that exist have been instituted by God. Therefore whoever resists the authorities resists what God has appointed, and those who resist will incur judgment. For rulers are not a terror to good conduct, but to bad. Would you have no fear of the one who is in authority? Then do what is good, and you will receive his approval, for he is God's servant for your good. But if you do wrong, be afraid, for he does not bear the sword in vain. For he is the servant of God, an avenger who carries out God's wrath on the wrongdoer. Therefore one must be in subjection, not only to avoid God's wrath but also for the sake of conscience. For the same reason you also pay taxes, for the authorities are ministers of God, attending to this very thing.

—ROMANS 13:1-6

Since God is, properly speaking, the only one who can claim absolute authority in Himself, lesser offices derive their authority from His. The text also speaks about the purpose of earthly governments: to punish wrongdoers, to "bear the sword." Moreover, the earthly governor is God's "servant," God's agent. In other words, just as God gives daily bread through the means of the farmer, He deals out punishment to evildoers and protects law-abiding citizens through the means of government authorities.

One of Luther's key writings on vocation was a pamphlet entitled *Whether Soldiers Too Can Be Saved*. Many Christians in Reformation times, in the first flush of discovering the Bible, maintained that since we are supposed to love our enemies, Christians should not serve in the military, which involves killing our enemies. Since we are supposed to forgive sinners, they reasoned, Christians may also not serve as judges, who instead have to punish them.

In response, Luther asked whether *God* is allowed to take a human life or to punish sin. Indeed, He is. Luther maintained that it is God, working through the *offices* of the judge or soldier, who takes life and punishes sin. Christians can indeed occupy these offices, being called to them as divine vocations. So a soldier is loving his neighbor when he protects his country, and a judge is loving his neighbor when he puts a criminal in prison or delivers him over to the executioner (another valid vocation).

And yet this by no means negates the commands to love our enemies and to forgive those who trespass against us. In their personal lives, soldiers, judges, and executioners must indeed love and forgive their enemies. But in their vocations, by virtue of their offices, they are authorized to "bear the sword."

Those of us who do not have that vocation, however, cannot

take the law into our own hands. Immediately prior to the
Romans 13 text, St. Paul expresses the Christian's duty to for-
give wrongdoing in terms just as strong as in the Sermon on the
Mount:

> *Repay no one evil for evil, but give thought to do what is hon-*
> *orable in the sight of all. If possible, so far as it depends on*
> *you, live peaceably with all. Beloved, never avenge yourselves,*
> *but leave it to the wrath of God, for it is written, "Vengeance*
> *is mine, I will repay, says the Lord." To the contrary, "if your*
> *enemy is hungry, feed him; if he is thirsty, give him something*
> *to drink; for by so doing you will heap burning coals on his*
> *head." Do not be overcome by evil, but overcome evil with*
> *good.*
>
> —ROMANS 12:17-21

We are not supposed to take personal revenge. We don't have
to. God will avenge us. And in the very next passage, we learn
how He does this: through the vocation of the governing authority, who is "the servant of God, an *avenger* who carries out
God's wrath on the wrongdoer" (13:4, emphasis added).

It must be remembered, though, that most ordinary vocations do not have this authority. When someone commits a
crime against us, we do not have to track down the wrongdoer.
We call the police. Though a father has the vocation of protecting his home, and though all citizens should resist evildoers (as
the hijacked passengers so bravely did on United Airlines Flight
93 that crashed in Pennsylvania), it is not up to us, as individuals, to bring global terrorists to justice. Our law enforcement
officials and our military do this on our behalf.

The social disorder that can come from acting outside of our
vocations is evident in the Americans who in the aftermath of
the September 11 attacks took it upon themselves to beat up

Arabs and to vandalize mosques, acts that were clearly sinful and unjust. A judge, as a private citizen, cannot slap an injunction on an annoying neighbor or order someone thrown into jail in a fit of road rage. The judge can only perform his office as he is authorized by the law. Police officers, soldiers, even Presidents and Congressmen must act in accord with an objective, formal code of law that ratifies them in their office and both grants and limits the authority they can exercise. Their authority resides not in themselves but in their office, and their office is a function of the law.

That nations have laws, just as God has laws, is another example of how the spiritual realm is, in a sense, hidden in the secular realm. The two kinds of law are not the same, one being earthly and social, and the other being transcendent and moral. Still, they are related. Human laws derive their authority from God's Law.

The state law against a vehicle crossing an intersection when the light is red is not, of course, written in the Bible. It is a human law in every way, time-bound (related to the invention of the automobile and the electric light), and a matter of convention rather than transcendent truths (since "red" meaning "stop" is just an arbitrary agreement, and any other color might have done as well). Christians, like every other citizen regardless of his or her faith or lack of it, are obliged to keep the law—not just because otherwise they will get a ticket, but because it does, ultimately, relate to God's moral law. There is no biblical commandment about stopping for red lights, but there is a command to love our neighbors. Obeying the traffic laws prevents cars from running into each other and people from getting hurt. Therefore, it is necessary to submit to the authorities "not only to avoid God's wrath but also for the sake of conscience" (Romans 13:5).

Some human laws are direct manifestations of God's Law, such as the provisions against murder and theft. Others, such as traffic laws, do have a divine moral principle behind them. God's Law, though, encompasses things human laws cannot. God's Law judges the inner recesses of the human heart. Human law simply regulates outward behavior. A "law-abiding citizen" may be the model of good behavior, according to the law of the land and the tenets of "civil righteousness," and yet in his heart be a damnable sinner in need of God's grace.

THE SUBMISSION CONUNDRUM

Romans 13 makes many Christians squirm. Are we *always* supposed to submit to our rulers? Does that mean we should not even criticize them? The issue is especially troubling when Christians live under bad or oppressive rulers. Were the Christians of Germany obliged to submit to Hitler and to participate in his murderous, blasphemous schemes? Many said "yes," citing this very Scripture. But are there not unjust laws, made by evil regimes, some directly contradicting the commandments of Scripture? For example, in the early church Roman law demanded that citizens burn incense as a way to acknowledge the divinity of the Emperor. Or more recently, the law in many Islamic states forbids anyone from trying to convert a Moslem to Christianity. Christian missionaries can be subject to the death penalty for telling someone about Jesus. Does Romans 13 mean that they should not evangelize the lost in nations whose leaders forbid it?

It is clearly not the calling of a ruler to oppress his people. His purpose, again, is to love and serve his neighbors—that is, his subjects. A good ruler will thus be one who works for their good. Specifically, he serves God and does good to his people by punishing wrongdoers: "For he is God's servant for your good. But if you do wrong, be afraid, for he does not bear the sword in vain. For he is the servant of God, an avenger who carries out God's wrath on the wrongdoer" (Romans 13:4).

It follows that a ruler who punishes those who do good is acting outside his vocation. One who bears the sword in vain, one who does *not* punish evil, out of either indifference or out of a false sense of kindness inappropriate for his office, is neglecting his calling. Those rulers who abuse their authority by using it for their own advantage—stealing from their people, enslaving them, forcing them to obey their whims for their own gratification—are sinning against their vocation. God calls a ruler to, paradoxically, "serve" his subjects, not to exploit them. He is also to be "God's servant." Presumably, even when he does not know the true God, as would be the case with the Roman ruler about whom St. Paul was writing, his vocation entails being God's "servant." When he refuses to serve God by fulfilling the purpose of his vocation, he will be held accountable for violating his stewardship.

Certainly human rulers do not always operate according to God's design for their office. Sin keeps spoiling every earthly institution. The Bible itself warns about the abuses that happen when a human being is given supreme legal authority. The Israelites, tired of being elect among the nations, which entailed being ruled directly by the Law of God, wanted instead to be like other cultures, having their own human institutions. They asked Samuel to appoint them "a king to judge us like all the nations" (1 Samuel 8:5). The prophet warned them what would happen:

> He said, "These will be the ways of the king who will reign over you: he will take your sons and appoint them to his chariots and to be his horsemen and to run before his chariots.

*And he will appoint for himself commanders of thousands
and commanders of fifties, and some to plow his ground and
to reap his harvest, and to make his implements of war and
the equipment of his chariots. He will take your daughters to
be perfumers and cooks and bakers. He will take the best of
your fields and vineyards and olive orchards and give them to
his servants. He will take the tenth of your grain and of your
vineyards and give it to his officers and to his servants. He will
take your male servants and female servants and the best of
your young men and your donkeys, and put them to his work.
He will take the tenth of your flocks, and you shall be his
slaves. And in that day you will cry out because of your king,
whom you have chosen for yourselves, but the* LORD *will not
answer you in that day."*

—1 SAMUEL 8:11-18

Nevertheless, the people wanted to have a king. So Samuel, *at
God's command and by His choosing* (8:22; 9:15-17), anointed
Saul to be their king. His reign was a failure, as were most of his
successors', and Samuel's prophecy about how their kings would
abuse them came true. Nevertheless, the office had been established by God, who used it for His purposes—from the building
of the temple to the establishment of the royal line that would
culminate in Jesus Christ, the King of Kings.

Much of the Old Testament consists of prophets excoriating
their lawful kings—for their idolatry, for oppressing the widows
and orphans, and for other violations of God's Law. That the
kings of Israel and Judah were under the higher Law of God—
and thus subject to criticism for their unrighteousness—is in
stark contrast to the way kings were construed in "all the
nations" of the ancient world. For the Canaanites and the
Egyptians and other cultures of the time, the king was divine.
Pharaoh was believed to be a direct descendant of the sun god.

The king was no mere human ruler but an actual deity. This was why he himself was the source of law. As Herbert Schneidau points out, it was conceptually impossible to criticize a monarch. There was no transcendent moral frame of reference above the king, by which he could be judged or his edicts questioned. In the pagan religions, nature, the cultural and political structures, and the gods were all one. Schneidau, in his book *Sacred Discontent: The Bible and Western Tradition*, points out how the Hebrew tradition, which placed kings under the transcendent authority of God, made possible both social criticism and social change.

Still, the Bible upholds the office. "Honor the emperor," says St. Peter after reiterating the principles of Romans 13 about submitting "to every human institution, whether it be to the emperor as supreme, or to governors as sent by him to punish those who do evil and to praise those who do good" (1 Peter 2:13-17). "The king's heart is a stream of water in the hand of the LORD," says the book of Proverbs; "he turns it wherever he will" (21:1). Again we have a precise metaphor for the way God providentially works His purpose through the vocation of the ruler.

Thus we have a paradox: Rulers are to be obeyed, yet they themselves must obey the higher Law of God. The notion that the king is under the Law would have the profoundest implications for Western civilization. Stanton Evans, in his book *The Theme Is Freedom*, shows how the theory and practice of political freedom derives directly from the biblical limits placed on kings, as developed throughout the Christian tradition, from the early church through the Middle Ages to the founding of the American Republic. Kings became subject not only to the laws of God, but to the laws of their own governments.

Again, it is the law that makes a ruler, that ratifies a person into the office, and that gives the office its authority. The New Testament passages requiring submission to the governing authorities were in the context of Roman law, which extended throughout the Empire. For all of the tyranny of the Roman emperors, one of the great positive contributions of Rome was its system of laws. Today's legal system, from property law to the legal rights held by citizens, is built on the foundation of Roman law, which in many ways is still in effect. Roman law really was a great achievement, a model of institutionalized justice. The Roman Republic solved the problem of pure democracy that plagued the Greek city-states with crowd-manipulating demagogues, by devising a system of representative government, with the Senate acting on behalf of the people, whose rights were protected by special advocates known as tribunes. In time the Republic was usurped by the emperors, though the Senate still functioned in local matters and still had to ratify the new emperors, who eventually made new laws by fiat and claimed divine status for themselves, a reversion to the practice of the other pagan cultures. But Roman law continued to function like a self-contained, well-oiled machine, even as it was extended with the imperial conquests throughout Europe and the Mediterranean world.

The superiority of Roman law to the lawlessness of the mob is evident in Scripture, for St. Paul himself appealed to his rights (and his calling) as a citizen of Rome. When he was attacked by the mob at Jerusalem, he was protected by the commander of the Roman garrison. When he was about to be flogged anyway, in an act of petty official tyranny, he asked the centurion, "Is it lawful for you to flog a man who is a Roman citizen and uncondemned?" Vocations, including that of citizenship, not only have duties—they have prerogatives; and Roman citizens had specific legal rights, including immunity from certain punishments and the right to the full protection from the law. "So those who were about to examine him withdrew from him immediately, and the tribune was afraid, for he realized that Paul was a Roman citizen, and that he had bound him" (Acts 22:25, 29).

In general, the laws of a society are a good thing, as opposed to the chaos of lawlessness. The calling of a ruler—whether an emperor, a king, a president, a governor, a mayor, or the vast array of judges, police officers, sheriffs, and other local officials who exercise authority in the government—is accomplished by a formal, rigorous legal procedure. Typically there is even an investiture of some kind, a swearing-in that marks the entering into the office. In the United States those who enter into these offices must swear an oath, often with their hands on the Bible, to uphold and defend the Constitution. That is, American rulers must put themselves under the authority of the law. Other societies too generally have something similar. The European kings are anointed by an official of the church. The Roman emperor was ratified by the Senate.

A dictator, by contrast, is someone who has seized power by force. No one elected the former Taliban regime that took over in Afghanistan, exiling the king and imprisoning opposition parties. Revolutions can be lawful or unlawful. The French revolutionaries guillotined their old rulers, abolished the law, and instituted a new legal system by force. The Communist revolution and the Nazi revolution installed regimes that were illegitimate, thus lacking any valid authority.

The American Revolution, by contrast, tried to build a legal case, grounded on the necessity of parliamentary representation and other rights of citizens as found in English law. The American Revolution was not resolved until the Treaty of Paris, in which the King of England himself granted the colonies independence. (Christians who worry that the United States government is not legitimate because the Revolution violated Romans 13 need not worry. The ruler himself agreed to let us go and, in the treaty he signed, assigned legal authority to the American legislatures.)

So is it ever right to disobey the authorities? In almost every circumstance a Christian should, in Peter's words, "be subject for the Lord's sake to every human institution" (1 Peter 2:13). There are rare times, though, in which a ruler acts outside his authority by violating either his nation's law or the higher Law of God. In this case the rulers no longer have a basis for their authority. They act outside of their calling. Sometimes a government might pass a law that violates the Law of God. Such a law can hardly claim divine authority.

Though the doctrine of vocation has been criticized for giving divine sanction to human rulers and the social roles of the status quo, the fact is, those who believed in this doctrine were not above fomenting revolutions of their own. The Reformation, while insisting on the duty of citizens to obey their rulers, managed to set the Lutheran princes against the emperor and inspired the English Puritans to overthrow their king. But these Reformation revolutions were put forth under the aspect of law, the long-established rights of the nobles that were being infringed by the emperor and the authority of Parliament established since the Magna Carta and threatened by King Charles I. The English Puritans were not just a mob of theocrats who stormed the palace; they were the duly elected representatives of Parliament. Though they might have gone too far in executing the king, they did not tear him limb from limb in an out-of-control riot; they put him on trial, for treason no less, for fighting against his own people. Genuine anarchy, such as happened with the Peasants' Revolt, was ruthlessly crushed—no doubt too ruthlessly—by the Reformation princes at the urging of their theologians.

In the words of a Reformation confession of faith, "Christians owe obedience to their magistrates and laws except when commanded to sin. For then they owe greater obedience to God than to human beings" (Augsburg Confession, Article XVI). The confessors cited Acts 5:29. When the disciples were forbidden by law to preach the Gospel, they answered: "We must obey God rather than men." Luther did believe that when it was necessary to disobey the authorities, Christians should be willing to accept the punishment. At a time when many rulers had made translating the Bible a crime punishable by death and had outlawed the proclamation of salvation through Christ alone, Christians endured martyrdom rather than obey a godless law. But they willingly accepted the consequences of their lawbreaking, and so managed to submit to the ruling authorities even at the cost of their lives.

CITIZENS OF A FREE COUNTRY

Just as there are many kinds of nations in the world, each with its own laws, there are many kinds of rulers. Emperors, kings, tribal chieftains—these are all offices Christians are enjoined to obey. There is another kind of ruler, though, the kind found in the United States and other democratic systems. This gives Romans 13 a special twist for Americans and others who live under a democratic republic. Our governing officials are not imposed on us from above. Rather, we elect our governing officials. Ultimately *we* rule *them*. In a democratic system the "people" rule. Their leaders are accountable to the citizens, who enact their own laws through their elected representatives and who are endowed by their laws with the task of self-government.

Those who have been blessed by a calling to live in the United States or another free country have a more complicated vocation of citizenship than do those who live under a monarchy. In a democratic society citizens are still subjects, but at the same time they are rulers.

An American president is, indeed, a "governing authority" to which we should submit; but he is by no stretch of the principles a king. We should submit to the office, in that we obey the laws he is supposed to execute, but he cannot require citizens to do whatever he commands. Our Constitution does not give him that power. He is neither the source of law nor the interpreter of law. The public elects the President from a field of candidates. Submission to his authority cannot include always voting for him. Nor can it mean refusing to criticize him. In our legal and political system, the people must assess the President's performance and that of other elected officials; otherwise it would be impossible to have a democratic republic.

Those called to be American citizens, therefore, have a Romans 13 obligation to take an active part in their government. Christians should indeed obey the laws, pay their taxes, and honor—and pray for (1 Timothy 2:2)—their governing officials. Feelings of patriotism and acts of civic-mindedness are fitting responses to the blessings God has given this country and to the citizenship to which He has called them. But the calling to citizenship also includes active involvement in their nation and in their government: voting, debating issues, grass-roots politics, and civic activism.

Christians who mobilize for pro-life causes—even when this means criticizing officials and working to change laws—are acting in their divine vocation as citizens. Christians who, like the prophets, challenge the evils in their societies, including those perpetuated by their officials or their institutions, are acting in their divine vocations as citizens. So are Christians running for the local school board, demonstrating at the statehouse, going to precinct meetings, and voting for the candidates who best reflect their beliefs.

This emphatically does *not* mean turning the church into a political action committee or confusing the spiritual work of the Gospel with the political arm of the state. Christian political activism falls under the vocation of citizenship—not the vocation of faith; and it is important, as shall be seen, not to confuse the different callings. But Christians are called to be engaged not just in government but in their cultures as a whole, working, through their various vocations, to make their country, if only in a small way, a better place for their neighbors.

CHAPTER EIGHT

Your Calling in the Church

§

Christians, then, have callings in their families, in their work, and in their communities. These are their vocations in the world. But they also belong to a spiritual family, have spiritual tasks, and are part of a spiritual community. That is to say, Christians also have a calling in the church, both as a spiritual kingdom and as a local institution.

Many Christians today are scornful of "the institutional church." They see its faults and its weaknesses, are distracted by the ordinary folks who make up the typical church, and are easily disillusioned with the way it operates. It is so "unspiritual," they think. Many, burned-out with the ever-failing quest to find the perfect church, think they can do without it or try to replace it with informal Bible studies or by throwing themselves instead into parachurch organizations. Others devise totally different ways of "doing church," only to create another institutional church of their own design.

But minimizing the ordinary local church is a great mistake. Christ is hidden in His church on earth, and always has been.

Just because He is not seen—just because there are no spectacular spiritual special effects or because those who worship Him in church are not religious superheroes—does not mean He is not present. He is where He has promised to be—in the Word of God, in the Sacraments, and with His people—"where two or three are gathered in my name" (Matthew 18:20).

Christ is also working, in a powerful way, through the vocation of the pastor. Christ, as He animates His Body, also works through what laypeople are called to do in the local congregation. All of those seemingly humdrum tasks—singing in the choir, serving as an elder, being on the board of trustees, teaching in Sunday school, doing committee work—are nevertheless critical areas of service that are tremendous blessings to the whole congregation.

CALLED TO FAITH

Being a Christian is itself a calling. That is to say, a person becomes a Christian by being called by God.

> *And we know that for those who love God all things work together for good, for those who are called according to his purpose. For those whom he foreknew he also predestined to be conformed to the image of his Son, in order that he might be the firstborn among many brothers. And those whom he predestined he also called, and those whom he called he also justified, and those whom he justified he also glorified.*
>
> —ROMANS 8:28-30

The verse about God's providential care is familiar and often quoted, but the rest of the passage tends to be left out of the quotation. In all things God works for the good of those *"who are called* according to his purpose" (emphasis added). The promise

that God will work things out for the good of His children has to
do with vocation. God's good "purpose" is being fulfilled in those
He has called. The next verses give another remarkable promise
related to vocation. "Those whom he predestined *he also called*;
those whom he called he also justified" (emphasis added).

Here is the whole nine yards—everything that pertains to
being a Christian. Foreknowledge, predestination, justification,
sanctification (being "conformed to the likeness of his Son"),
glorification. These are presented not separately but together.
And what links them is being "called." Someone who has been
"called" has them all.

The various terms here are taken differently by different theological traditions, and this is not the place to launch into a discussion of exactly what predestination, for example, entails.
Discussing these terms in isolation from each other might be part
of the reason they can become so confusing. Some people, for
example, worry whether they have been predestined. But this
Scripture should calm any such fears. Were you called? Then you
were predestined. Were you called? Then you were justified.
Were you called? Then you will be glorified and will enjoy everlasting life.

But what does it mean to be "called"? Elsewhere St. Paul
goes over the same ground but is more specific about what the
call consists of:

> *But we ought always to give thanks to God for you, brothers*
> *beloved by the Lord, because God chose you as the first fruits*
> *to be saved, through sanctification by the Spirit and belief in*
> *the truth.* To this he called you through our gospel, *so that*
> *you may obtain the glory of our Lord Jesus Christ.*
> —2 THESSALONIANS 2:13-14,
> EMPHASIS ADDED

He called you—to this state of being chosen, to this salvation, sanctification, and belief—by means of *the Gospel*.

To "call" someone literally means to address that person in human language, usually with a loud voice. To "be called" means to hear that voice. "My sheep listen to my voice" (John 10:27).

When St. Paul speaks of "calling," as he does so often, he is not being metaphorical. He means that we are addressed personally by the Word of God. In a passage directly parallel to this text—in his *first* epistle to the Thessalonians, in the very same chapter and verse—the apostle unpacks what this means: "And we also thank God constantly for this, that when you received the word of God, which you heard from us, you accepted it not as the word of men but as what it really is, the word of God, which is at work in you believers" (1 Thessalonians 2:13). Not only did the Thessalonians hear, receive, and accept the Word of God, but that Word "is at work in you." It does something. "The word of God is living and active" (Hebrews 4:12). "My word . . . that goes out from my mouth," says the Lord through His prophet, "shall not return to me empty, but it shall accomplish that which I purpose, and shall succeed in the thing for which I sent it" (Isaiah 55:11).

That purpose includes bringing us to repentance through the condemnation we realize when we are confronted by our failure to keep God's Law; and it includes bringing us God's grace when we hear the Gospel, the good news of our forgiveness in Christ. "The gospel," says St. Paul, "is the power of God for salvation to everyone who believes" (Romans 1:16). The Gospel is such that, through the power of the Holy Spirit, it creates faith in our hearts, just as God spoke the universe into existence. "God is faithful," says St. Paul, "by whom you were

called into the fellowship of his Son, Jesus Christ our Lord"
(1 Corinthians 1:9).

A Christian, then, is someone who has heard and believed the
Gospel—that is to say, someone who has been called to faith by
the Word of God. The calling is not just a subjective experience,
nor some inner voice. Rather, it comes from outside the self, to
the self. It is language, the Word of God, specifically the message
that tells about Jesus dying for your sins. The first time you may
have heard this from a friend witnessing to you. You may have
heard the call to faith as you read the Bible or a tract. You may
have heard this Gospel in a sermon or by having been immersed
in Scripture as you were growing up.

Os Guinness, discussing the meaning of the biblical term,
observes that "to call means to name, and to name means to call
into being or to make" (as in Genesis when God *called* the light
"day") (30). It is often said that a Christian has been called in
his or her baptism, in which the person is named, whereupon
that name is joined to "the name of the Father and of the Son
and of the Holy Spirit." To be baptized is to be personally joined
to the death and resurrection of Christ. "Do you not know that
all of us who have been baptized into Christ Jesus were baptized
into his death? We were buried therefore with him by baptism
into death, in order that, just as Christ was raised from the dead
by the glory of the Father, we too might walk in newness of life"
(Romans 6:3-4).

The call to faith—received in the message of the death and
burial of Christ and the rebirth of baptism into Him—marks the
beginning of the Christian life. But Christ keeps calling us to
Himself every time we read God's Word or hear God's Word
proclaimed or receive the Lord's Supper and listen to its words,
"This is my body, *given for you.*"

Some people may brush off all of these words; but others, for one reason or another, are pierced to the heart by the message of Jesus. "My sheep hear my voice, and I know them, and they follow me" (John 10:27).

CALLED OUT

Because Christians are called by God's Word, they are called *out of* the sinful world and *into* the Church. This is most eloquently stated by St. Peter: "But you are a chosen race, a royal priesthood, a holy nation, a people for his own possession, that you may proclaim the excellencies of him who called you out of darkness into his marvelous light. Once you were not a people, but now you are God's people" (1 Peter 2:9-10). With the call of God, the person who was once an isolated and alienated sinner becomes part of a holy nation, the people of God, an actual community whose purpose is to declare the praise of the Caller. That is, the Christian becomes a member of Christ's Church.

The word translated *church* in the Greek New Testament is *ekklesia*, which derives from the particle *ek*, meaning "out," added to the verb *kalein*, meaning "to call." The verb *ekkalein* means "to summon or to call out." As Os Guinness reminds us, the New Testament word for *church* means literally "the called out ones" (30). The Church, the *ekklesia*, is the assembly of those who have been called.

This "holy nation," of course, extends back through time, just as being a citizen of a regular nation means being a part of its history. The company of all of the redeemed is a spiritual reality, comprising all the denizens of Heaven now and in the future. But it is also a community that lives here and now on earth. Christians will feel an affinity for their fellow believers wherever they are, especially when they find them out in the secular world or in a common vocation. They will find a particular unity and sense of belonging with those whose theology they agree with, the collection of congregations that make up a denomination or a particular theological tradition. But the church that a Christian belongs to will, above all, be a specific congregation.

Sometimes Christians feel a conflict between the Church, as a spiritual organism that transcends time and place, and their local congregations. The latter can seem so ordinary, so blasé, so "unspiritual." But Christians are sometimes so spiritually minded they forget that their faith has to do with the tangible, material, real world. C. S. Lewis, in *The Screwtape Letters*, has a devil discussing how to distract a Christian by emphasizing the mundane appearance of an ordinary local congregation:

> When he goes inside, he sees the local grocer with rather an oily expression on his face bustling up to offer him one shiny little book containing a liturgy which neither of them understands, and one shabby little book containing corrupt texts of a number of religious lyrics, mostly bad, and in very small print. When he gets to his pew and looks around him he sees just that selection of his neighbours whom he has hitherto avoided. . . . It matters very little, of course, what kind of people that next pew really contains. You may know one of them to be a great warrior on the Enemy's side. No matter. Your patient, thanks to Our Father Below, is a fool. Provided that any of those neighbours sing out of tune, or have boots that squeak, or double chins, or odd clothes, the patient will quite easily believe that their religion must therefore be somehow ridiculous. At his present stage, you see, he has an idea of "Christians" in his mind which he supposes to be spiritual but which, in fact, is largely pictorial. His mind is full of togas and sandals and armour and bare legs, and the mere fact that the other people in church wear modern clothes is a real—though of course an unconscious—difficulty to him. Never let it come to the surface; never let him ask what he expected them to look like. (4-5)

These ordinary folks, coming together to worship their God, may not look like anything special, but in reality they are part of the Church "spread out through all time and space and rooted in eternity, terrible as an army with banners" (4).

In all of the ordinariness of a local church and an average Sunday morning worship service, Christ—as with other vocations, though this time in a spiritually saving way—is hidden. He is actually *there* wherever two or three are gathered in His name (Matthew 18:20). He is present in His Word and in His Sacraments and in the hearts of all believers who, though drab and lowly and nothing special on the outside, make up nevertheless a royal priesthood whom Christ has called and in whom He dwells.

CALLED AND ORDAINED

Hearing the voice of Christ is equivalent to hearing God's Word. Christians gather into churches for one reason—because they hunger and thirst for that Word. "So faith comes from hearing," says St. Paul, "and hearing through the word of Christ" (Romans 10:17). This truth is carried out, once again, through a human vocation:

> But how are they to call on him in whom they have not believed? And how are they to believe in him of whom they have never heard? And how are they to hear without someone preaching? And how are they to preach unless they are sent?
>
> —ROMANS 10:14-15

That God calls people through His Word means there is a need for preachers—also, for people to send preachers.

The vocation of the pastor is a special office indeed. Not that it is more meritorious than any other vocation. God acts and is hidden in other vocations as well. But the pastoral office serves not just the world but God's spiritual kingdom. Christ is active in the pastor's work in a saving way, giving the pastor's words and ministry eternal consequences.

Just as God raises children through families, gives daily bread through farmers, heals through doctors, He nurtures, feeds, and heals—on the spiritual level—through the vocation of the ministry. Christ proclaims His forgiveness of sins through the lips of a pastor. It is Christ who is preaching, baptizing, presiding at His Supper, and in the deepest sense "ministering" to His people, through the earthen vessel of the pastor.

This is not just mystical symbolism but a plain fact. Again, the call to faith is a matter of God's Word. A pastor's obligation is to preach not his own opinions but the Word of God. Typically he has spent years in seminary studying the Bible. A sermon is an exposition and an application of Scripture. In his teaching the pastor is involved in explaining and communicating effectively what the Bible says. His goal—and I think any good pastor would say this—is to be a clear channel for the Word of God. Certainly he may not get it totally right, and his own prejudices and personality may get in the way—though Christ is able to work despite such imperfections; but the pastor's message, his purpose, and his authority consist of nothing more than God's Word.

A pastor has no particular calling to expound from the pulpit his political opinions or to discuss his favorite movie or to share an interesting article from *Psychology Today*. These may be interesting to the congregation or not. What he is called to do from the pulpit is to proclaim God's Word. He might bring in politics or a movie or that interesting article, but only as illustrations or explanations or applications of what God has to say in Scripture. Similarly, in his teaching, counseling, visitations, and the thousands of other things pastors find themselves doing, from weddings to funerals, their mission is to bring the Word of God—not just the Law but preeminently the Gospel of Christ—to bear on the lives of their parishioners.

The risen Lord told His disciple Peter to "feed my sheep" (John 21:17). The word *pastor* means "shepherd." The pastor is someone who tends the often unruly and oblivious sheep that make up the congregation, feeding them with the Word and Sacraments, protecting them from the wolves of false teachers, seeking the lost, and leading his flock to the green pastures of everlasting life. Of course, Jesus Christ Himself is the real Shepherd—the Good Shepherd who lays down His life for the sheep, the One whose voice the sheep recognize (John 10:1-16); so He is our true pastor. But just as our Heavenly Father makes use of earthly fathers, the Lord as our Shepherd makes use of earthly shepherds. Christ carries out His shepherding, in large measure, through the vocation of the pastor.

A division of labor took place within the church in its earliest days. The book of Acts tells about two specific church vocations:

> *Now in these days when the disciples were increasing in number, a complaint by the Hellenists arose against the Hebrews because their widows were being neglected in the daily distribution. And the twelve summoned the full number of the disciples and said, "It is not right that we should give up preaching the word of God to serve tables. Therefore, brothers, pick out from among you seven men of good repute, full of the Spirit and of wisdom, whom we will appoint to this duty. But we will devote ourselves to prayer and to the ministry of the word."*

—ACTS 6:1-4

In this terminology, all of the Christians are called "disciples," but the Twelve—those schooled by Jesus Himself—exercised a leadership role in the church. It is surely significant that the church was concerned for the physical needs of its members, particularly its widows, who had no one else to care for them. Here and elsewhere in Acts we see that the church is a community of faith—not just a place to go for an hour on Sunday morning, but a place where Christians are involved in each other's lives. And yet this was no idealized utopian commune where all of the Christians were loving each other all of the time. Rather, even the church led by the twelve original disciples had its friction, in this case ethnic conflicts and that perennial complaint, "That's not fair!"

In any event, the twelve disciples found themselves spending so much time on the practical details of administration—getting the food together, keeping track of who gets what, "serv[ing] tables"—that they were neglecting their major vocation, namely, "preaching the word of God." Moreover, because of all of the complaints about the inequity in the food distribution, they were not doing a very good job with their administrative tasks. Running the church's food program was evidently not their vocation. So the church elected seven qualified laymen to handle the practical, even secular matters the church was dealing with, so that the Twelve could spend their time in "prayer and the ministry of the word."

Today many congregations have adopted secular business models for the running of their churches. The pastor, some are saying, is the chief executive officer of the church-as-corporation. He has his corporate board (the board of elders) and his executive staff; the various specialized "ministries" are answerable to an organizational chart. His workers are the laypeople of the congregation, who are organized into various task forces.

What the company is selling is the Gospel, and the goal is to market the Church's message to attract the religious consumers out in the world. The job of the pastor/C.E.O. is to administer the physical plant and the budget, set policy, be the visionary leader, and equip everyone under him for ministry.

Business models can be great for businesses, and being a C.E.O. is a worthy calling in its sphere. But the Church is not a secular institution but a spiritual one, and the call of a pastor has a specific content and is not reducible to just leading an institution. As we shall see in a later chapter, vocations must not be confused with each other, and acting outside of one's calling is a formula for disaster.

One pastor told me that he has not done an evangelistic call in years. He has a committee of laypeople to do that. Nor has he done any hospital visitations. He organized a group of laypeople to visit shut-ins and people in the hospital. Laypeople lead all of the Bible studies and Sunday school classes. They conduct prayer groups and plan the worship services. Though his members are busy, he does not waste their time by letting them have a say in what the church does. He said that he has not had any congregational meetings for years. He makes all the decisions. He does preach sometimes, though he takes turns with the other ministers on staff. What he mostly does, he explained, is *organize* all of these different groups, set policy, and oversee the physical plant.

In other words, he has laypeople do what *he* has been called to do—evangelism, caring for his flock—while he is doing what *laypeople* are called to do—handle the day-to-day, practical institutional details. He is reversing Acts 6: He is "serv[ing] tables." The members of his congregation are doing "the ministry of the word."

Both groups are acting outside of their vocations. This is

usually a formula for ineffectiveness. One wonders how good his committees are at evangelizing the lost, or if they really know what to say when visiting the sick and the dying in the hospital, or, lacking seminary training, how good a job they do teaching the Bible. Or how good this pastor, with his seminary training rather than an M.B.A., is as a C.E.O. I do not know specifically, but many churches organized along these lines are struggling with severe financial problems and are notorious for dysfunctional employee relationships and communication breakdowns.

Certainly laypeople in the church are to be equipped for witnessing to their faith and other tasks common to all Christians. Of the seven deacons in Acts 6, Stephen was a powerful spokesman for the faith, to the point that he was arrested by the Sanhedrin and was sentenced to be stoned to death, becoming the first Christian martyr. Another, Philip, proclaimed Christ in Samaria, performed miracles, and opened the Scriptures to the Ethiopian eunuch (Acts 8). Laypeople are especially positioned to reach people *outside* the church, by virtue of their secular vocations, which put them in contact with people who would never darken the door of a church.

But pastors, whose calling is specifically to preach the Gospel, to feed Christ's sheep, and to study and to teach God's Word, will be particularly blessed when they realize that in their ministry Christ is ministering through them.

THE BODY OF CHRIST

There are many different church polities, different ways of organizing and governing the church—congregational, presbyterian, episcopalian, and various combinations and variations of these—and different theologies about the office of the Holy

Ministry. Those are beyond the scope of this book; and besides, not being a pastor myself, to discuss them in any kind of informed way is outside my vocation.

There are many different denominations and different theological traditions, each with its own characteristic beliefs and practices. I do not consider this a bad thing. This may be a shocking thing to say in this ecumenical age. Don't I believe in Christian unity? Yes, I do, and the need for unity in a church is precisely why I believe in many denominations. Christians should join together in worship with those whose faith and theology they share. The members of a congregation need to be unified. If a church body embraces many different theologies and practices, there will be a lack of unity. It is far better, in my opinion, to have a diversity of churches than to have a diversity of theological positions within a single church, a condition that can only lead to vagueness, inconsistency, and confusion of teaching. But how can any one tradition claim to have the whole truth? Well, believing in something means to believe that it is true. Each Christian should be in the church that he or she thinks has, as close as possible, the whole truth—that is, the best understanding of Scripture.

The church is to be both unified and diverse. All who have saving faith in Jesus Christ are united with each other, even those from different theological traditions, in which, though they may contain certain errors, the Word of God can still create faith in the hearts of those who are called. The Reformation refers to the "invisible church," the company of believers, hidden though they may be, known by God. But there must also be the visible church, the actual congregations, which may contain both saints and hypocrites, all of whom are nourished by Word and Sacrament in a tangible, localized community of faith. These are typically made up of many dif-

ferent individuals from all walks of life, from every social class
and profession, each with a unique personality. Each can take
a part in the love and service of the fellow members that make
up the life of the church.

St. Paul explains the points of unity and the points of difference in one of the most remarkable passages in Scripture:

> *For just as the body is one and has many members, and all the*
> *members of the body, though many, are one body, so it is with*
> *Christ. For in one Spirit we were all baptized into one body—*
> *Jews or Greeks, slaves or free—and all were made to drink of*
> *one Spirit.*
>
> —1 CORINTHIANS 12:12-13

As he says elsewhere, "There is one body and one Spirit—just
as you were called to the one hope that belongs to your call—one
Lord, one faith, one baptism, one God and Father of all"
(Ephesians 4:4-6). All Christians, whatever their ethnic group or
their social status or their vocations, share a common baptism
into the name of the Father, Son, and Holy Spirit. There is only
one Holy Spirit, who has brought us to faith and continues to
minister to us through God's Word. There is one Christ and one
Father. There is only one call, that of the Gospel of Christ.

Having established this unity, the apostle goes on to laud the
diversity of those who share this baptism and this faith:

> *For the body does not consist of one member but of many. If*
> *the foot should say, "Because I am not a hand, I do not belong*
> *to the body," that would not make it any less a part of the*
> *body. And if the ear should say, "Because I am not an eye, I*
> *do not belong to the body," that would not make it any less*
> *a part of the body. If the whole body were an eye, where*
> *would be the sense of hearing? If the whole body were an ear,*

where would be the sense of smell? But as it is, God arranged
the members in the body, each one of them, as he chose. If all
were a single member, where would the body be? As it is,
there are many parts, yet one body.

—1 CORINTHIANS 12:14-20

Not only is Christ hidden in the unassuming members of the
local church, but He calls them His Body. Christians are unified
in Him, but their differences from each other are the differences
that are necessary within any living organism.

That the eye is utterly unlike the ear does not mean they are
unrelated. Indeed, since they are part of one body, they have an
intimate connection, a union with each other. "If one member
suffers, all suffer together; if one member is honored, all rejoice
together" (v. 26).

This is all a prelude to the apostle's breakdown of the different
tasks and gifts—the different vocations—within Christ's Church:

Now you are the body of Christ and individually members of
it. And God has appointed in the church first apostles, second
prophets, third teachers, then miracles, then gifts of healing,
helping, administrating, and various kinds of tongues. Are all
apostles? Are all prophets? Are all teachers? Do all work mir-
acles? Do all possess gifts of healing? Do all speak with
tongues? Do all interpret?

—vv. 27-30

He goes on, in the famous chapter 13, to urge the quality that
all Christians should have—namely, love. But here he describes
various roles within the Church that are taken up by different
members equipped to perform them.

Many of these are performed in the pastoral office; some are
delegated to others. The "spiritual gifts" are perhaps best under-

stood not in terms of some extraordinary powers zapped into a person by the Holy Spirit, but in terms of vocation. That is, they are avenues for service, ways to love and serve one's neighbor—in this case, the other members of one's church. "There are varieties of service, but the same Lord" (12:5). They are gifts to be offered in the spiritual sphere that is the Church. They are not about authority or turf or rights, but about building up fellow believers (1 Corinthians 14:12).

To use a more mundane example, consider what the church musician does—the organist or the choir director or those who sing in the choir. The Old Testament describes how music was used in the worship that took place in the Tabernacle and the Temple:

> *The priests stood at their posts; the Levites also, with the instruments for music to the* LORD *that King David had made for giving thanks to the* LORD—*for his steadfast love endures forever—whenever David offered praises by their ministry; opposite them the priests sounded trumpets, and all Israel stood.*
> —2 CHRONICLES 7:6

David offered praise by the ministry of the musicians. Their playing and their singing helped *David* offer praise. So it is in a church service today. The organist and the choir help the rest of us offer our praises. They express our thanks for God's mercy for us, as it were, and with us and on our behalf.

Similarly the boards and committees, the Sunday school teachers, the trustees, the elders, the ushers, and the altar guild are all doing their part to serve one another and their fellow members, building up with the pastor the complex, living thing that is the church.

Yes, the church is an institution like any other earthly institution. It has its mortgages and sewer costs; it has to obey zoning regulations and fire codes. A church will have its bylaws and Robert's Rules of Order to govern its tedious but necessary meetings. The practical matters of management and administration will still apply. Members who have vocations in the secular arena can be a big help for churches trying to navigate their way through the world. Personality conflicts and communication breakdowns, unfortunately, will still happen, as in any large group of people. And yet this mundane institution is also the Body of Christ.

CHAPTER NINE

The Ethics of Vocation

༄

The doctrine of vocation is not just a teaching about the value of work. It comprises a theology of the Christian life. How are Christians to live in the world? What does a faithful Christian life look like as faith bears fruit in works? It is more than just being nice, and it is even more than doing the momentary heroic deeds of self-denial or of helping people. The life of vocation is comprehensive and day-by-day, involving almost every facet of our lives, the whole texture of relationships, responsibilities, and focuses of attention that take up nearly every moment of our lives.

Good works, for the most part, are done in vocation. Sin, too, takes place in vocation, in the myriad ways we violate our callings. Approaching moral issues from the perspective of vocation can illuminate *why* certain actions are right or wrong. The vocational angle can also help us understand what our duties are in our various jobs and social roles and, just as important, what the limits and boundaries are in what we are called to do. It also illuminates what we are *not* called to do.

What surprises some Christians is that when all is said and done, the specific responsibilities of vocation are not any different, from the outside, for Christians or non-Christians. A Christian construction worker or a Christian physician does pretty much what a good non-Christian in those fields must do. The difference is on the inside, as faith—or the lack of faith—makes a difference in the meaning of those tasks and in the way they become acceptable to God. The doctrine of vocation brings the spiritual life, literally, down to earth.

SINNING AGAINST VOCATION

It is, of course, possible to sin in vocation. In fact, in the Reformation manuals for self-examination to help bring repentance for one's sins, it is recommended that the penitent consider his various vocations in light of the Ten Commandments. As Luther recommends in his "Small Catechism," in preparing to confess one's sins to the pastor, "Here reflect on your walk of life in light of the Ten Commandments: whether you are father, mother, son, daughter, master, mistress, servant; whether you have been disobedient, unfaithful, lazy, whether you have harmed anyone by word or deed; whether you have stolen, neglected, wasted, or injured anything" (360). The model confession he gives is pungently earthy and grounded in the tangible, everyday world of vocation:

> "In particular I confess to you that I have not faithfully cared for my child, the members of my household, my spouse to the glory of God. I have cursed, set a bad example with indecent words and deeds, done harm to my neighbors, spoken evil of them, overcharged them, and sold them inferior goods and shortchanged them," and whatever else he or she

has done against the commands of God and their walk of life, etc. (361)

The catechism, studied, memorized, and internalized by generations of Lutherans to this present day, also includes a "Table of Duties," consisting of relevant Bible passages "for all kinds of holy orders and walks of life": "For Bishops, Pastors, and Preachers" (1 Timothy 3:2-4, 6a); "Concerning Governing Authorities" (Romans 13:1-2, 4b); "For Husbands" (1 Peter 3:7; Colossians 3:19); "For Wives" (1 Peter 3:1, 6); "For Parents" (Ephesians 6:4); "For Children" (Ephesians 6:1-3); "For Male and Female Servants, Day Laborers, Workers, etc." (Ephesians 6:5-8); "For Masters and Mistresses" (Ephesians 6:9); "For Young People in General" (1 Peter 5:5-6); "For Widows" (1 Timothy 5:5-6); "For All in the Community" (Romans 13:9; 1 Timothy 2:1) (365-367). Again, all of these are understood as "holy orders." Reformation catechesis placed vocation at the very center of ethical teaching.

One way to look at sin is as a violation of one's calling. Since the purpose of vocation, as has been seen, is to love and serve one's neighbor, failure to do so is a sin against one's vocation.

A political ruler who does not love and serve his people but exploits them for his own pride, greed, and lust for power—who uses his authority and the people under his care for his own selfish ends—is sinning against his vocation. God did not put him into this position for his own self-gratification. God is not hidden in acts of oppression. Though the authority of his office remains, the ruler who misuses that office is subject to the judgment of God.

Every vocation has its unique temptations and capacity for sin. Police officers are called to protect their fellow citizens, not to beat them up. Businesses are not given their callings to cheat their customers. Craftsmen doing shoddy work, journalists who write lies, artists who squander their talent by making pornography—such uses of God-given abilities to *hurt* one's neighbors, rather than to love and serve them, are sins against vocation. Parents are called to take care of their children, not abuse them. Husbands are called to love and care for their wives, not to mistreat them. Anything that violates the purpose of one's vocation—teachers are to teach, doctors to heal, parents to nurture—is not of God.

Consider some of the controversial moral issues we face today. Is euthanasia right or wrong? Well, a doctor's vocation is to bring healing. The purpose of his calling is not to kill people but to try to make them better. When a physician kills, he is violating his calling.

What about abortion? Doesn't a woman have the right to decide whether or not she wants to have a child? But when a woman becomes pregnant, she is called to motherhood. The mother's vocation is to conceive new life and to nurture her child as it grows. No mother is called to kill her child, nor does any physician have a calling to kill the child at her request. Neither of them has that authority.

What about sexual morality? Again, sex is authorized by the calling of marriage. Though it may seem strange to speak this way, you have no *authority* to have sex with someone you are not married to. Can there be homosexual marriage? Since the purpose of sex and the vocation of marriage is to engender new life, there can be no such calling.

What about the new reproductive technologies? *In vitro* fertilization may be appropriate within the vocation of marriage—when the sperm and the egg that are joined in the petri dish belong to the husband and the wife—but inappropriate when using a sperm donor to whom the woman is not married. The latter takes reproduction outside the vocation of marriage. The anonymous donor is ignoring his calling to fatherhood that comes with conceiving a child, neither knowing nor caring about the human being he has fathered. What about the use of surrogate mothers, in which a woman conceives a baby for another couple? The mother who conceived and bore the child has a calling to that child, a calling that cannot be broken by simply giving the child away, much less by selling it. And yet a single mother who gives up her child to adoption by a married couple, rather than getting an abortion, *is* loving and serving her neighbors (both her baby and the adopting couple) by bringing her child into the vocation of a full family, which she does not have.

THE LICENSE OF VOCATION

It is already apparent from these examples that vocation has the capacity to *authorize* certain actions, and that some things are right when done *inside* of vocation, but wrong when done *outside* of vocation. The very same action can be right or wrong, depending on the vocation of the person doing it.

For example, taking a knife and cutting a person open is a serious crime. But when a surgeon cuts a person open—that is, when he is doing it in his vocation as a way to love and serve his neighbor—he is doing a good work. The surgeon is authorized to use his scalpel by virtue of his office, with all of the training, skill, and official licensing that goes along with his vocation. If I, though, were to attempt to do surgery on someone, I would be arrested, and rightly so.

A judge may punish a criminal, even sentence him to death. We in the general public do not have that authority. We do not have that vocation. The executioner administering the lethal injection is not committing murder. We would be, if we tried to avenge wrongdoing by ourselves. The soldier who kills an enemy as an authorized member of the armed forces is not sinning. This is his vocation. He himself, though, is not allowed to kill his own personal enemies, those he is angry at for his own reasons. He has no license to kill outside of his vocation. Again, it is the office that has the authority, not the person who holds that office. And it is God who works in and through that office. As private individuals, the judge, the executioner, and the soldier are to live out radical ethical love as expounded in the Sermon on the Mount (Wingren, 7-8).

To go from violence to sex, once again husbands and wives, by virtue of their vocation of being married, are authorized to have sex with each other. They are not authorized to have sex with anyone outside of this vocation. The same sexual acts are good works within marriage, but sinful outside of marriage.

Parents have the authority to discipline their children. That is their vocation. As a rule, outsiders do not have this prerogative. The state is entitled to keep order, and citizens of the community can keep social order by giving dirty looks or by expressing an opinion; but it is the parents' job to keep a rowdy child in line, not that of an annoyed bystander. Parents sometimes assign some of their rights and duties to other vocations, such as teachers (to educate and, when necessary, to discipline their child) and ministers (to help them bring up their children in the faith). But the responsibility for the physical, intellectual, and spiritual well-being of their child belongs to the parents.

Sometimes parents resent schools or state agencies for presuming to raise their children for them. They are right to do so. It is the parents' vocation, not that of the government, to take care of their children. Schools that teach values contrary to those of the parents are acting out of their proper jurisdiction.

Different vocations are permitted to do different things. Nonauthorized personnel are not allowed on the shop floor. They are liable to get hurt or to hurt other people. It is not their job to be there. The vocation itself—along with the skills, the training, and the knowledge that go with a particular calling—gives both responsibilities and prerogatives, boundaries and freedoms.

ACTING OUTSIDE OF VOCATION

When we act outside of our vocations—that is, when we try to do something we have no calling for—we are only creating trouble for ourselves. Sometimes this may involve a moral transgression, as in taking the law into our own hands instead of calling the police or having sex with someone we are not married to. More often, acting outside of vocation is morally innocent, but it results in ineffectiveness, frustration, and wasted time.

I am hopelessly inept with my hands. Nevertheless, out of some American ideal of self-sufficiency, the conviction that a liberal arts major should be able to do anything, and congenital cheapness, I used to always try to fix things around the house. Invariably, after spending hours better spent elsewhere, I would botch up the job. Once I tried to fix an electrical outlet—how hard could it be?—and nearly got myself killed.

That was before I discovered the doctrine of vocation. I have no calling that would authorize or equip me to deal with electrical wiring. The knowledge involved is complex and highly technical, requiring skills that I just do not have. Now I call an electrician. I gratefully depend on those with specialized vocations who are willing to serve me, as their neighbor, with their God-given callings.

To be sure, some people *are* handy around the house—that

is part of their unique gifts and calling; but when we try to operate outside of what we have been called and gifted to do, we are engaged in an exercise of futility. I would have done much better spending my time writing or grading papers or playing with my kids or going out with my wife—things I *do* have a calling to do.

Sometimes we are pulled away from our callings by our own good intentions or those of other people. Os Guinness quotes the English writer Dorothy L. Sayers, famed for her mystery stories, her literary scholarship, and her Christian apologetics. Once she became famous, she would often be asked by clergymen to give talks, to appear at church functions, and to play the role of the Christian celebrity. This kind of thing, she believed, took her away from her real vocation, which was writing. "How dare they talk about Christian vocation," she complained, "when at the same time they try to take me away from my vocation, which is to be a craftsman with words, to waste my time doing something for which I have no vocation and no talent, merely because I have a name" (180).

We indeed have a calling to serve in our local churches, but it must be emphasized that our so-called "secular" vocations are actually "holy offices" where we are to serve our neighbors and live out our faith. "If you do your household chores," Luther told the servant girls, "that is better than the holiness and austere life of all the monks" ("Large Catechism," 406).

Churches should not demand so much "church work" from their members that it takes away too much time from their primary vocations. There was a time when I would spend nearly every evening at church—at Bible studies, committee meetings, evangelism calls, and other worthy activities. I was doing so much church work that I was neglecting my work (all of those papers to grade) and, especially, my family. (Pastors of churches, too, need to remember that they have a vocation not just in the office of the ministry but also as husbands and fathers. Congregations must take care not to overload their pastors to the point that they have to neglect their other vocations.) It may be that churches often try to do too much. We may assume that what happens on Sunday mornings is not enough, as if coming into Christ's presence through the proclamation of His Word is a small thing, and as if the daily lives of ordinary Christians are not themselves arenas for divine service.

A woman told me about getting involved in a Bible study that demanded strict commitment to the study of God's Word. "You should make the Bible your number one priority," she was told. That meant getting up early and the very first thing in the morning doing Bible reading and having a quiet time with the Lord. She did this, but to her consternation every morning as she would start to read her Bible, the baby would wake up. She found herself resenting the interruption. Here she was, trying to spend time with God, and the baby would start fussing, demanding to be fed and distracting her attention away from spiritual things. After a while, though, she came to understand the doctrine of vocation. Taking care of her baby was what God, at that moment, was calling her to do. Being a mother and loving and serving her child was her vocation, her divine calling from the Lord. She could read the Bible later. She did not have to feel guilty that she was neglecting spiritual things; taking care of her baby *is* a spiritual thing!

GOD AT WORK DESPITE OURSELVES

However much we sin in and against our vocations—and we sin a great deal—God is at work in them. It is God's love that is active in vocation, and though we may try to thwart it in our sinfulness, and though we make ourselves obstacles to God's will, He works in what we do despite ourselves.

"Even persons who have not taken the gospel to their hearts serve God's mission, though they be unaware thereof," says Wingren, "by the very fact that they perform the outer functions of their respective stations" (7). But those who have received the Gospel have the joyous confidence that their access to God does not depend on either their works or their sins, but on the free gift of Jesus Christ. Christians, by faith, can know that God is working in them and through them.

As Luther tells the servant girl, if she can be made to realize the truth about vocation, she "would dance for joy and praise and thank God . . . with her careful work, for which she receives sustenance and wages, she would obtain a treasure such as those who are regarded as the greatest saints do not have." "How could you be more blessed or lead a holier life," he asks her. "In God's sight it is actually faith that makes a person holy; it alone serves God, while our works serve people. Here you have every blessing, protection, and shelter under the Lord, and, what is more, a joyful conscience and a gracious God" ("Large Catechism," 406-407).

CHAPTER TEN

Bearing the Cross in Vocation

§

The doctrine of vocation is utterly realistic. And a part of realism is to acknowledge the hardships, the frustrations, the failures that we also sometimes encounter in our vocations. Yes, work can be satisfying and fulfilling, but—sometimes at the same time—it can be arduous, boring, and futile. Yes, it is wonderful to have children, but they can also break a parent's heart. Yes, marriage is a blessing, but there are also sometimes fights, arguments, and emotional roller coasters. Yes, it is good to love one's country, but citizenship becomes a burden when the leaders are corrupt and the laws are unjust. Yes, we cannot do without our church, but sometimes it is maddeningly frustrating in the way it operates.

Our vocations, like the rest of the earth, are under a curse, one directed explicitly at marriage, childbirth, and work (Genesis 3:16-19). Adam and Eve were driven out of Paradise, and a cherubim keeps us out with a flaming sword (3:22-24); so we can expect no utopia, no perfect nation, and no perfect congregation. And yet the Seed of the woman did come, and though the Serpent bruised His heel, He crushed the Serpent's head (3:15). Jesus did remove the curse, though we remain in its shadow; but He did so by suffering and dying for us on the cross.

Luther's doctrine of vocation is tied in with all of the other facets of his theology—justification, sanctification, the means of grace, the Two Kingdoms; and he also relates it to his pastoral teachings about suffering. We have already discussed the hiddenness of God as it relates to vocation. God hides Himself, above all, in His incarnation, when He came not, as we might expect, as a king or a mighty warrior or some other glamorous vocation. Rather, He came first as a homeless child to a poor family who laid Him in a manger. When He grew up, despised and rejected among men, He was crucified, assuming the station of a criminal executed by the state. And yet through this humiliation and suffering, endured by God's own Son, He won our salvation.

Luther distinguishes between what he calls "the theology of glory" and "the theology of the cross." We naturally yearn for "glory," for success, victory, and living happily ever after. We thus prefer religions of glory, ones that promise us a successful life, that answer to our full rational satisfaction all of our questions, that grow and thrive, becoming ever more popular and powerful.

The problem is (to our human minds), God saved us by means of the Cross. The Christian life He gives us is the Way of the Cross. "If anyone would come after me, let him deny himself and take up his cross daily and follow me" (Luke 9:23). This cannot refer just to another martyrdom, as experienced by many of His disciples; nor is it just some "thorn in the flesh" that Christians must put up with. It is something that must be borne "daily."

Whatever this entails—the pattern of repentance and forgiveness that makes up the texture of the Christian's life; the persecutions and rejections, bitter or mild, that a Christian will experience; the physical suffering and eventual death that no one can escape—it also relates, Luther thought, to vocation. Though personal and unique for each person ("take up *his* cross"), the Way of the Cross means that our spiritual life does not consist solely of victories, miracles, and success stories. To be sure, God sometimes refreshes us with victories, and glories of every kind await us in the everlasting life that He has prepared for His people. Jesus died, but then He rose again and ascended into Heaven, and the next time He will come, as the creed says, "with glory." So there is glory in the Christian life, but in the meantime we must bear our crosses. And when we do, we find that we are driven to depend on Jesus more and more. Our prayers intensify, we cling to His Word, and our faith grows deeper and deeper as we find that Jesus, who bore our sufferings as well as our sins (Isaiah 53:4), takes up our crosses into His cross.

TRIALS IN VOCATION

It is not just sin that gives us trouble in vocation. We face trials. We face tribulations. Sometimes we experience utter failure.

Two parents bring a child into the world, care for him, raise him up, nourish him on God's Word. And yet when he grows up, he rejects everything he has been taught, everything the parents have stood for. They have had a calling to form and love this child, but he goes astray from it all. They torment themselves with questions: Did we fail as parents? What should we have done differently? What can we possibly do to get through to our son?

A businessman builds a company, providing goods and services to the public, employing scores of workers. This is his calling, and he is good at what he does. But then the economy turns. He has to lay people off. He tries, but he cannot save his business. He goes bankrupt. He thinks, *What about my calling now?*

A pastor has been called by a congregation. He has served them faithfully, teaching them God's Word, proclaiming the Gospel, baptizing them, feeding them with the Lord's Supper, pouring himself out for their spiritual growth. And then they turn against him. Maybe for some trivial reason—they want a different kind of music; or a family has its feelings hurt and is now trying to drive him out of their church—or maybe for something more serious, such as rejecting the message He has been called to convey. *Didn't God call me here?* he wonders. *Why didn't my ministry do any good?*

Failures in vocation happen all the time. Wise statesmen find themselves voted out of office. Noble generals lose the war. Workers lose their jobs, maybe because they are not good at what they do, despite what they thought. Sometimes even good, competent, skilled workers with a clear calling get laid off because of a hiccup in the stock market over which they have no control. People who think they have a calling as a writer cannot get published. What once seemed to be good, healthy marriages start to implode.

Even people who by many standards would seem, from the outside, to be successful in their vocations nevertheless consider themselves failures. *This is not what I really want to do,* they think. *I should be doing a lot better. No one appreciates me. What good is it all?* Os Guinness gives the example of Mozart, one of the most obviously gifted geniuses of all time, who reportedly considered himself a failure (125-129).

Sometimes the trials are less dramatic. Sometimes we are

wearied with our vocations. We get burned-out. The satisfaction is gone, leaving behind just the tedium. Shakespeare said it well, probably referring to his own magnificent vocation of writing poetry: "with what I most enjoy contented least" ("Sonnet 29").

These are crosses to bear. They have no easy answer or solution. If they did, they would not be crosses.

TEMPTATIONS

Sometimes trials are temptations. "Temptation in vocation," says Gustaf Wingren, "is the devil's attempt to get man out of his vocation" (121). That is to say, since God has called a person to a vocation, the Devil's strategy is to try to make him quit.

A husband and wife in a troubled marriage will be tempted to get a divorce rather than to work out their problems. A frustrated artist will be tempted to stop practicing his art. An easy way out of a difficult job is to quit. A pastor in a difficult church will be tempted to give up his ministry. This impulse to give up on one's calling, according to Wingren, is from the Devil.

To be sure, some failures—such as being unable to do well in a job and so losing it—are a result of not having a calling after all. To get laid off or fired or to lose one's business, or otherwise losing one's vocation in a way that is outside your control, may mean that you are being called to something else. Sometimes the pastor of a troubled church will do well to exercise his divine calling at another congregation. But to reject one's own God-given calling—such as breaking up a family by getting a divorce and letting the children the couple were to nourish fend for themselves—can only be the work of the Devil (though Christ can forgive that, like all sins).

An even more insidious temptation, though, can come from

success. "Wanting to be exalted instead of serving, regarding office as a possibility for selfish power instead of for service, is offense against vocation," says Wingren. "The natural man is always aspiring to rise out of lowliness to the heights; he follows his evil bent to get away from serving. Through the very action of striving upward toward honor and self-complacent splendor, he separates himself from the living God, who in sacrificial love bows down to created things and stands close to all who are in the depths. This man forsakes his neighbor, so he lives not with God but with the devil who leads him away from the path of his vocation" (128-129).

In other words, the Devil tempts the holder of a vocation to the way of glory. Insisting on being served rather than serving, the calling becomes an occasion to wallow in pride. The mentality this creates is one of self-sufficiency. The person in this vocation feels no need for dependence on God. There is certainly no need for the Gospel, since the person in this successful position is doing just fine by himself. The Devil has twisted the vocation so that it undermines both love for neighbor and love for God.

In contrast, the Christian uses vocation as an occasion to serve, which in itself is humbling and self-denying. But this is how God loves and serves, the Way of the Cross. According to Wingren, citing various passages from Luther:

> God's action is determined by his self-proffering love, which seeks the lost and the fallen. For to Luther God himself, when he is described as Creator, becomes utterly like a human being faithful to his vocation, who gives himself to the lowly. God creates out of nothing, i.e. he gives heed to the despised and helpless who are at the point of death. In the crucifixion of Christ on Golgotha, he who was despised by the world showed himself a true Creator, one who makes his costliest

work out of that which is nothing. A Christian is therefore also a person who is ever in desperation, need, and weakness, since he is that *nihil* [that "nothing"] out of which God creates. (129)

Trials and tribulations, even failure, keep Christians aware of their weakness, aware of their utter dependence on God. And it gives them empathy for their neighbors in need and a desire to serve them out of love.

This does not mean that suffering is some sort of "good work" or means of grace. There is no merit in suffering in vocation, any more than there is merit in the ascetic self-inflicted pains of the monasteries. Luther makes clear that crosses are never self-chosen. That is, choosing to flog oneself is not a cross, nor is choosing a course of action that you know will get you into trouble, just for the self-righteousness of being persecuted. Crosses we choose are not crosses. Things that go against our will—one might say, things that cross our will—are the crosses we have to bear. These do not have to be major afflictions. The small, mundane annoyances of life may serve just as well.

If, as has been said, God hides Himself in vocation, He hides Himself, as at Golgotha, in its crosses. But how is the hidden God found? What should Christians do when they experience trials and tribulations and temptations in their vocations?

PRAYER IN VOCATION

The answer, given by the Reformation theologians, is that suffering drives us to prayer. "He who labors knows that there are times when all human ways are blocked," observed Wingren. "In a special sense this is the time for prayer" (185). For Luther, our prayers are most intense and genuine when we are at our wits' end, when problems press themselves upon us to the extent that we give up, when in our desperation there is literally nothing that we can do. At that lowest point, in prayer, we throw ourselves completely upon the Lord. "For what sort of prayer would it be if need were not present and pressing upon us," asked Luther, "that prayer be thereby the stronger?" (*The Sermon on the Mount* [1532]; quoted in Wingren, 189).

What prayer does is to bring God into our vocations. Of course, God operates in them without our prayer. But as Luther's catechism says of the fourth petition in the Lord's Prayer, "God gives daily bread indeed without our prayer, also to all the wicked; but we pray in this petition that He would lead us to know it, and to receive our daily bread with thanksgiving." That is, prayer can lead God to intervene in our situations. But prayer also affects *us*. When we so much as ask for our daily bread, it is not that our prayer makes God give it to us, as though if we did not pray we would starve for lack of food. Rather, God in His mercy to all the world provides our daily bread, working through the natural order and, specifically, through vocation. God gives daily bread even to the wicked. But when we pray, we "know it"—we realize, with an increasingly thankful heart, that it is God who is feeding us.

When we pray, we recognize our dependence on Him, and we turn ourselves over to His will. When we pray in our vocations, we recognize their connection to God—to His will, His judgments, and His grace. We have said that God is hidden in vocation. In prayer, we get a glimpse of Him. The mask is lifted.

"Prayer is the door," says Wingren, "through which God, Creator and Lord, enters creatively into home, community, and labor" (194). When we try to fulfill our vocations without prayer, he says, we are in effect (as far as we are concerned) shutting Him out from our work. "Therefore vocation, which involves the total

of a person's relationships and his situation, can be properly fulfilled only by constantly renewed prayer" (192).

We pray for our needs in our vocations—whether the problem is in the family or the workplace, the community or the
church—and God answers in terms of our vocations. He may
indeed intervene to resolve the problem. We may come to see the
problem as an intimation of His wrath and judgment, moving
us, in conjunction with God's Word, to repent and to seek His
forgiveness; or we may realize that we need to forgive those in
our vocation who have trespassed against us. But however God
chooses to answer our prayers, whether by changing the situation or by changing us, we have given the outcomes over to Him.

Our part is to carry out our vocations. The outcome belongs
completely to the Lord. The burden is shifted over to Him.

Fathers and mothers are to carry out their callings as parents, to fulfill their station however imperfectly but with the
help of God and constant prayer. They have done their part.
The rest they must leave in the hands of God. If their child,
grown up, goes wrong, they need not torment themselves. They
have carried out their vocation. But they will never cease praying for their child, clinging to the hope that when a child is
trained in the way he should go, "*when he is old* he will not turn
from it," however much he turns from it until then (Proverbs
22:6, emphasis added). When the child grows up, even when
the child is headed in the right direction, parents, having dis-
charged their vocation to conceive and to care for their child,
can only turn him or her over to the Lord and whatever He
chooses to do with them.

Something similar happens when a Christian starts a business (which may go bankrupt) or runs for office (the campaign
may be defeated by a landslide) or enters into any other venture—a pastorate, a battle, a marriage. Occupy your office with

prayer. The results and consequences and outcomes are largely beyond your control. But they are not beyond God's control. Realizing that one does not have to worry about what will happen, that the future is in God's hands, is liberating. Again to quote Luther, who runs through a whole list of vocations:

> Work and let him [God] give the fruits thereof! Rule, and let him prosper it! Battle, and let him give victory! Preach, and let him make hearts devout! Marry, and let him give you children! Eat and drink, and let him give you health and strength. Then it will follow that, whatever we do, he will effect everything through us; and to him alone shall be the glory. (*Exposition of Psalm 147* [1532]; quoted in Wingren, 194)

God is working through what we do in vocation. We are merely His instruments. When we realize that, we can relax.

While we are quoting Luther, it might be fitting to quote his vocation prayer, from his *Commentary on the Sermon on the Mount*:

> Dear Lord, I have Thy Word, and I am in the station that pleases Thee. This much I know. Thou seest all my inadequacies, and I know no help except in Thee. Help Thou, therefore, because Thou hast commanded that we should ask, seek, knock, and hast said that then we shall surely receive, find, and have what we need. (232-233)

The promises of God's Word and the conviction that right now, where I am, I am in the station—the vocation—where God has placed me—those constitute the basis for confidence and certainty that God has assuredly placed me here and that He is faithful and that He, even though I cannot see Him, is at work in and through my life.

FAITH IN VOCATION

The kind of dependence upon God realized in prayer, particularly when facing trials and tribulations in vocation, is a manifestation of faith. As we trust Christ for our salvation, so we come to trust Christ in every facet of our daily lives—our vocations—so that, in bearing our crosses, we rely more and more on His cross, and we grow in faith.

It is *faith* that transforms suffering into a cross. "There are times," observes Wingren, "when, by the will of God, failure, defeat, obstacles, and bitter things befall us." But "troubles and tribulations are to drive us closer to God; they benefit rather than harm us" (234).

For the person without faith, on the other hand, "life's bitterness is actually something evil. It testifies to God's wrath and hands man over to Satan's power, for he is constantly given to impatience, ill feeling and egocentricity. Through tribulations he is led not to heaven but to destruction" (235-236). The problem of evil really is a stumbling block to those who have no faith in Jesus Christ, and their hardships lead them further and further from God and deeper into their lost condition.

Luther's approach to theodicy is not to offer yet another explanation as to why God allows evil, but to distinguish between how suffering is perceived from the perspective of unbelief and from the perspective of faith—that is, the perspective of the Cross. It is not just suffering. All of life, all of vocation, is transfigured by faith or is darkened by its absence:

> This faith creates rest, satisfaction, and peace and dispels weariness. But where faith is lacking and man judges according to his own feelings, ideas, and perception, behold, weariness arises. Because he feels only his own misery and not that of his neighbor, he does not see his own privileges nor how

unfortunate his neighbor is. The result of this unsatisfied feeling is aversion, trouble, and toil throughout life. He grows impatient and quarrels with God. God is not praised, and there is no love or gratitude to God. . . . He embitters his life, and hell is his reward. Here you see how faith is necessary in everything; how it makes all things easy, good, and pleasant, even in prison or in death, as the martyrs prove. But without faith all things are difficult, bad, and bitter, even if all the pleasures and joys of the whole world were yours, as is shown by all the mighty and the rich, who live the most miserable life all the time. (*Kirchenpostille* [1522], quoted in Wingren, 236)

This does not mean that faithful Christians are happy all the time—far from it, since they must bear their crosses—nor that unbelievers are always unhappy. Since the latter do not have a cross to bear, they may well have an easier time of things than Christians. The point is, faith gives an inner meaning to what would otherwise be experienced as meaningless.

Two carpenters, side by side, are doing the same job, one a Christian and the other an unbeliever. Their work, on the outside, is exactly the same. Both are following the same calling, with its rules, techniques, and demands. They may even think of their vocations in the same way, whether as just a way to make a living or feeling the satisfaction of creative work well done. There is not a "Christian" way to be a carpenter, as opposed to being a non-Christian carpenter. Nevertheless, one fulfills his vocation in faith, while the other rejects God and prefers to be completely on his own.

One day the scaffolding falls. Both are injured. Both are suffering horribly. They are side by side in two hospital beds. They are feeling exactly the same misery. The Christian, when he can, prays in agony. He is not healed, but he exercises his faith. The unbeliever feels not only the suffering but the meaninglessness of his suffering. He resents the God he does not believe in.

They both get better. They go back to work. One has grown closer to his God. The other, embittered, has grown farther away—unless at the point of his helplessness he has started listening to his coworker, who has been trying to tell him about Christ for years.

CHAPTER ELEVEN

Conclusion:
Resting in Vocation

❦

The doctrine of vocation offers a theological way of thinking about work. In its attention to institutions such as family and government, it also offers a theological way of thinking about society and culture. Recovering the doctrine of vocation can help Christians influence their culture once again as they carry their faith into the world, into its every nook and cranny, through the plenitude of vocations.

The doctrine of vocation is a theology of the Christian life, having to do with sanctification and good works. It is also a theology of *ordinary life*. Christians do not have to be called to the mission field or the ministry or the work of evangelism to serve God, though many are; nor does the Christian life necessarily involve some kind of constant mystical experience. Rather, the Christian life is to be lived in vocation, in the seemingly ordinary walks of life that take up nearly all of the hours of our day. The Christian life is to be lived out in our family, our work, our community, and our church. Such things seem mundane, but this is because of our blindness. Actually, God is present in them—and in us—in a mighty, though hidden, way.

THE VOCATION OF BEZALEL

The first explicit treatment of the doctrine of vocation in the Bible was on Mount Sinai. Moses had received the Ten Commandments, and God revealed to him how He desired to be worshiped. Since the sacrifices of blood required elaborate altars, basins, and a mysterious Ark of the Covenant, and since the worship was to take place in a Tabernacle reflecting the heavenly court itself, someone had to be able to make all of these things:

> *The LORD said to Moses, "See, I have called by name Bezalel the son of Uri, son of Hur, of the tribe of Judah, and I have filled him with the Spirit of God, with ability and intelligence, with knowledge and all craftsmanship, to devise artistic designs, to work in gold, silver, and bronze, in cutting stones for setting, and in carving wood, to work in every craft.*
> —EXODUS 31:1-5

God called Bezalel to the vocation of being an artist. This was a personal calling—he was "called by name"—and then he was equipped with gifts from God so he could carry out God's purposes for his vocation.

In another book, *State of the Arts*, I argue that the specific gifts mentioned in Exodus are, in fact, the gifts necessary for any good artist and any good work of art: ability, intelligence, knowledge, and craftsmanship. Each is indispensable. Together they constitute God's gifts for the arts. When God ordained "artistic designs" for His Tabernacle, He called and equipped an artist.

Bezalel, being "filled . . . with the Spirit of God" (the first person in the Bible of whom this is said), had also been called to faith. But the text says that God also filled him with ability, intelligence, knowledge, and craftsmanship. These were evidently not supernatural powers zapped into him miraculously, but personal talents and aptitudes that he already had in the natural course of things. They are still described as being the work of God.

This calling was not restricted to Bezalel alone. God also "appointed with him Oholiab." And not just him either: "I have given to all able men ability, that they may make all that I have commanded you" (v. 6). Later, when Moses announced these offices and this work to the people, other Israelites flocked to the project to help them build what God directed. They too are described as being "called": "And Moses called Bezalel and Oholiab and every craftsman in whose mind the LORD had put skill, everyone whose heart stirred him up to come to do the work" (Exodus 36:2). A sign of their calling was their own interests. The would-be artist's "heart stirred him up" to take part in the work, whereupon Moses called him.

LIVE AS YOU ARE CALLED

Another important biblical text for the doctrine of vocation is when St. Paul enjoins the Corinthians, "Only let each person lead the life that the Lord has assigned to him, and to which God has called him" (1 Corinthians 7:17). Our calling is not a choice out of many options but rather an assignment.

Each one should remain in the condition in which he was called. Were you a slave when called? Do not be concerned about it. But if you can gain your freedom, avail yourself of the opportunity. For he who was called in the Lord as a slave is a freedman of the Lord. Likewise he who was free when

called is a slave of Christ. You were bought with a price; do
not become slaves of men. So, brothers, in whatever condition
each was called, there let him remain with God.

—1 CORINTHIANS 7:20-24

On one hand, it does not matter—not to God—whether you are
a slave or a free citizen. Those called to faith through the Gospel
now have a life of freedom, no matter how their society treats
them. And even the free are slaves under the authority of Jesus
Christ.

Some people criticize the doctrine of vocation for establish-
ing a static social order. If God works through the established
magistrates, that serves to give divine sanction to human political power. If God calls you to be a peasant, the assumption is,
then you must never try to improve your lot.

The best answer to that is to see what impact the doctrine of
vocation did, in fact, have on society. The Reformation was a
catalyst for unprecedented social mobility, as education for Bible
reading and the vocation-inspired "Protestant work ethic"
spurred former peasants into an entrepreneurial middle class,
leading eventually to political as well as economic freedom.
Those called to be magistrates remained under the greater
authority of God's Law and could be criticized accordingly, a
notion that would soon lead to republican self-government.

This Scripture too, though often interpreted as freezing the
social order, in fact speaks against it. When you were called—
that is, called by the Word of God into faith—were you a
slave? St. Paul says not to be concerned about your low social
status, but he immediately goes on to say that if you can gain
your freedom, do so. The whole passage in fact undermines the
very basis for slavery of every kind: "You were bought with a

price," the blood of Christ, our true Master; "do not become slaves of men."

In the context, St. Paul has been discussing the vocation of marriage, sexual relations and the authority the husband and wife have over each other's bodies, whether believers should get a divorce from unbelieving spouses, and the like. When he says to live as you were called, he is saying, among other things, do not change your various callings just because you became a Christian. If you were married when you first believed the Gospel, do not divorce your unbelieving spouse. Your original calling is still valid. If you were a Gentile pagan when you became a Christian, do not get circumcised and make yourself a Jew (vv. 18-19). Stay what you are.

Certainly the early church made gladiators give up their profession, which was not a legitimate vocation because it involved not loving and serving their neighbors, but killing them for sport. The Gospel hurt the trade of the silversmiths who made idols of Artemis (Acts 19:21-27). But for the most part new converts remained in their original callings. Lydia kept selling purple dye. Paul kept making his tents. Zacchaeus remained a tax collector, though he stopped embezzling from the take and paid back the taxpayers he'd cheated. Converts kept the same families, made their livings in the same way, remained citizens of the same nations.

The application of this text for today seems to be, first, that we should indeed accept our callings as having been assigned to us from the Lord. This means being secure in our state—not wanting to be something or someone we are not—recognizing it as a gift and an office from the hand of God.

It also means that a new Christian should, for the most part, remain in his calling. Many converts to Christianity today, especially if they are celebrities, immediately launch off into some "ministry." It is not necessary for them to express their laudable zeal in this way. Let them remain musicians or movie stars or sports heroes. When spiritually immature Christians jump into a demanding ministry, it can be like a child trying to drive—dangerous to both others and themselves. Stay in your callings, St. Paul tells them. You can serve God and your neighbor where you are.

Later, with long study and experience in the Christian life, these people might mature into capable spiritual leaders. They might receive another calling to do that. Indeed, while we may have a calling to our place of work, we may very well receive another calling to somewhere else. The slave in the text might have the opportunity for freedom. A worker slogging away faithfully in his vocation may get the chance for a better job. Again, the call of God may come through a job offer, a proposal, or an election. Since vocations are multiple and are in the here and now, the calling to be a student might be supplemented by a calling at a fast-food restaurant. Upon graduation, the calling may be to a stock brokerage on Wall Street. In each case, he can be confident in God's purpose for his life and be in a position where he can love and serve his neighbors. At every stage he is leading "the life that the Lord has assigned to him, and to which God has called him."

REST FROM ONE'S CALLING

The Bible tells us to work; it also tells us to rest. We are to pause from our work to worship God on the Sabbath Day. In vocation, we are to rest in Christ even when we are hard at work.

Once when I talked about vocation in a church, an elderly man plaintively asked, "What about me? I'm retired! Don't I have a vocation?" Even though he no longer had to go to work, he still had vocations. He had a wife, grown children, and grandchildren. He was active in his church. He was active in politics. It turned out he had a number of hobbies—called "avocations," meaningful and often creative occupations that one does not do to make a living—which he employed to love and serve his neighbors.

But retirement from a lifelong vocation can be difficult, especially for those with Protestant work ethics. Properly, though, the laying down of a vocation after many years of work is a kind of Sabbath, a kind of reward for service rendered. The Puritan writer John Cotton says it well:

> The last work which faith puts forth about a man's calling is this: faith with boldness resigns up his calling into the hands of God or man; whenever God calls a man to lay down his calling when his work is finished, herein the sons of God far exceed the sons of men. Another man when his calling comes to be removed from him, he is much ashamed and much afraid; but if a Christian man is to forego his calling, he lays it down with comfort and boldness in the sight of God. (Quoted in Guinness, 243)

Whether God is calling him to work or calling him to refrain from working, it is all God's gift. And when we face our last calling, the summons to die, we can lay down our lives at the foot of our Master, who, having been at work in every other one of our vocations, is at work in this, to bring us to Himself.

There is another kind of rest in our calling. William Powers, a nuclear physicist at the national laboratory in Los Alamos, New Mexico, was asked how being a Christian affected his work. He explained how abstruse is his research into theoretical physics, how it consists mainly of working at a computer screen, analyzing thousands of calculations, tracking the behavior of obscure subatomic particles with infinitesimal half-lives.

He said that while he finds this work fascinating and though it is indeed useful in the field of nuclear energy research, he used to worry about the value of what he was doing. He wondered, *What good is this really?* He felt he should be spending his time doing something that was of more service to the Lord, such as evangelizing, instead. But ever since he learned about the doctrine of vocation, he feels a new satisfaction in his work. In his number-crunching and theory-testing, in exercising his abilities as a scientist, he knows he is leading "the life that the Lord has assigned to him, and to which God has called him." He is confident that in his office as a scientist, in his vocation, he is doing God's work.

Bibliography

Augustine, Saint. *Confessions*. Trans. Henry Chadwick. New York: Oxford University Press, 1991.

"The Augsburg Confession." In *The Book of Concord: The Confessions of the Evangelical Lutheran Church*. Eds. Robert Kolb and Timothy J. Wengert. Minneapolis: Fortress Press, 2000.

The Book of Concord: The Confessions of the Evangelical Lutheran Church. Eds. Robert Kolb and Timothy J. Wengert. Minneapolis: Fortress Press, 2000.

Evans, M. Stanton. *The Theme Is Freedom: Religion, Politics, and the American Tradition*. Washington, D.C.: Regnery, 1994.

Guinness, Os. *The Call: Finding & Fulfilling the Central Purpose of Your Life*. Nashville: Word, 1998.

Lewis, C. S. *The Abolition of Man*. New York: Macmillan, 1947.

—————. *The Screwtape Letters*. New York: Bantam, 1982.

Luther, Martin. "Commentary on the Sermon on the Mount." In *Luther's Works*, Vol. 21.

—————. "The Large Catechism." In *The Book of Concord: The Confessions of the Evangelical Lutheran Church*. Eds. Robert Kolb and Timothy J. Wengert. Minneapolis: Fortress Press, 2000.

—————. "The Small Catechism." In *The Book of Concord: The Confessions of the Evangelical Lutheran Church*. Eds. Robert Kolb and Timothy J. Wengert. Minneapolis: Fortress Press, 2000.

Sayers, Dorothy L. *The Mind of the Maker*. Westport, CT: Greenwood Press, 1941.

Schneidau, Herbert. *Sacred Discontent: The Bible and Western Tradition*. Berkeley, CA: University of California Press, 1977.

Shideler, Mary McDermott. *The Theology of Romantic Love: A Study of the Writings of Charles Williams*. New York: Harper, 1962.

Wingren, Gustaf. *Luther on Vocation*. Minneapolis: Fortress Press; rpt. Evansville, IN: Ballast Press, 1994.

Scripture Index

General Index